Two-Way Street

An American Success Story

Eric Soda

Spilled Coffee Publishing—Neenah, WI
ISBN: 979-8-218-24214-5
Library of Congress Control Number: 2023913180
Title: *Two-Way Street: An American Success Story*
Author: Eric Soda
Digital distribution | 2023
Paperback | 2023

"Do not go where the path may lead, go instead where
there is no path and leave a trail."

-Ralph Waldo Emerson

Contents

Introduction

For years clients and peers have asked me to share with them how I got where I am.

They've been pushing me to write a book. People think my story is interesting and inspirational. So that's exactly what I decided to do.

This book is scratching the itch that I never got to scratch. There wasn't a book like this when I was young and starting out. Nothing combined the ideas, tips, or insights on business and life into one book. Some tried but they just skimmed over things at a 10,000-foot view. They hinted at the tools, but never dove in and showed how to do things from start to finish. From A to Z. How did it work for them? How did they figure it out?

I started out in the insurance business while in high school in my hometown Princeton, Wisconsin, population 1,200. I didn't even know how to send a fax. From never getting a college degree, to being a firefighter, to starting an insurance agency at the age of 21, to setting sales records and becoming one of the largest agency owners for a Fortune 500 insurance company.

By age 32, I grew my insurance agency to be one of the largest captive insurance agencies in the country. We set the record for most life insurance policies sold in a year in American Family Insurance's 90-year history.

We've been nationally recognized for our achievements and sales records. I present to business owners all over the country on ways to improve their sales, service, and overall operations.

I've written this book in a way I'd like to read it. I've shared the life stories that shaped me and that also gave me perspective. If I was starting my business out again from the start, what would I want to know? What programs, tips, or ideas would I have wanted to know before opening the doors. How would I prepare personally and mentally? How would I get ahead and then stay ahead?

I've always looked at owning a business as a two-way street. That means that everyone involved is equally responsible for arriving at the desired destination. Both the client and the business work together to build and grow long term relationships established in trust and respect.

These teachings and tips are relatable to anyone and any type of business. The more I share, the more likely you find something that puts you ahead and gets you off on the right foot. Failure and falling on your face is important. Don't forget that! Because you will, just like I did. But the more knowledge and skills you can gain, the more educated, smart risks you can take to be great.

Please use this book as a tool. Take my successes and failures and build upon them. Use my failures as a learning experience so you don't make the same mistakes along the way.

This book isn't just for you. This book is for my kids. This book is for my future grandkids. You will see that this book is not just about business. This book is about life. It's about the business owner and entrepreneur as well as the person. This contains hard-hitting truths about life. Truths that you will need to know. Truths that maybe you have also experienced.

Much of what I learned throughout my life has ended up connecting like a puzzle. Life is complex, confusing, and hard, but it connects to help you both personally and professionally.

We learn from those that came before us. We learn from those who have run the race. I'm passing that on. If you have the chance, do it.

If all that follows in this book helps one person, then to me it's a success. All the time is worth it if I can impact one person's life. I hope that is you.

Part 1
Caring for People

1

My Firefighting Life

Beep! Beep! Beep! My pager let off a series of tones. There was a car on fire next to a house on the southeastern part of Princeton, Wisconsin, near the lake.

Into my truck I got. As I turned it on I could feel the adrenaline pumping through my veins. I've experienced it many times. Your blood is flowing so much that your leg starts to jump almost uncontrollably. Usually this happened when I drove the fire engine to a call.

When a notification comes across like this, where someone's home could go up in flames, it makes you kick into another gear. "Get your ass moving, Eric," I muttered to myself.

As I dashed across the street into the fire station to grab my gear, I hopped in the fire engine, the sirens blared, and George, our chief, laid on the air horn to clear traffic, I knew this would be my last fire call.

I had been on hundreds of calls, between fires and accidents. I'd hardly ever missed any. The insurance office in Princeton I was working at was just down the road from the fire station. Day or night I would answer the call to a fire or accident.

Now, the agency I was starting, and where I would be living, was an hour away. I was out of the district and not able to make calls anymore. I just wasn't around the area unless I was visiting or home for the holidays. That meant no more "rubbing dirt and breaking shit," as my firefighter buddies would say.

I sat smiling as I looked over at my firefighter brothers, who to this day remain close friends. If they or I ever need anything, even though we're an hour away from each other, we would all drop whatever we were doing to help one another.

This is a brotherhood that I've never experienced outside of the Princeton Fire & Rescue Department in my hometown. The brotherhood of firefighters is unlike any other. I grew up with these guys. They all knew my parents, grandparents, and family. Many even served in the department with my dad, uncles and grandpa.

It was about coming together for the situation at hand. When you call the fire department it is always in great need. I pulled dead people of all ages from car wrecks. I've helped search the charred remains of homes for missing parents and children.

The smell of a perished body is a smell that you never forget. It lives with you. It's not something you want to relive, but it does become a part of you. It puts life in a clear perspective. When you think you're having a bad day, you don't have to look too far to be thankful. These were life lessons that remain as clear as the afternoon sky.

Helping people was the name of the game.

I don't write a lot about my time as a firefighter. Many to this day don't know about it. I did the training necessary to go full-time, but it wasn't a career I wanted to pursue.

What it was though, was my childhood dream. Not many people get to check that box in life. At age 18, I was able to do something I had dreamed of doing since I was a little boy. I'd watched my dad, uncles, and grandpa leave family gatherings to go to fire calls.

I often think back to those years. It's a time that I relished. Now with a wife and kids, I doubt I'd ever do it again. But just like wanting to play one more snap of football, I'd give anything to suit up in SCBA again and go into a burning building. It is a feeling that is impossible to describe unless you do it. The adrenaline is unlike anything I've ever experienced.

Those guys who became brothers will still call me and we'll talk about what is new and usually end up reliving our days together fighting fires.

I bring up this part of my life because it was me. It's me to this day. There isn't a more gratifying job. It isn't glorious work. It is some of the hardest I have ever done.

I loaded people fighting for their lives from car wrecks into the med flight helicopter. I've helped assist cops in tackling criminals who were resisting arrest.

To this day, my ears perk up when I hear sirens. It doesn't matter what city or state I'm in. The thoughts and adrenaline start again. I wonder what's going on and who needs help.

Firefighters, police, and paramedics run towards trouble while others are running away. They never know exactly what they're in for. Every day their heroic efforts are just another day on the job. Just think about what those brave men and women all did on 9/11.

A batter must make a split-second decision whether

to swing or not. A quarterback has a split-second decision of whether or not to throw that pass. Firefighters, police, and paramedics have similar decisions to make. In those split seconds they must make a decision between life and death, not just for them but for others as well.

The next time you see these heroes, appreciate, and thank them. Unless you experience life in one of these heroic jobs, you'll never fully grasp what it is they go through from one day to the next. Give thanks to them.

Lessons Learned Being a Firefighter

Being a firefighter isn't a story that's told very often. There isn't a lot of good things about it that you want to remember. The duties are responding to people when they're in their greatest point of need. People dying or severely injured in car wrecks and families losing their homes and possessions aren't things you want to relive. It's tough. It's never easy.

When I'd drive the fire engine to an accident or fire, I never knew what I was going to come upon, who was going to be in the cars, who was going to be trapped in the house, or who's house you were going to be pulling up to. It created an adrenaline-pumping fear of the unknown that nothing can compare to.

Being a firefighter is about helping people. It's why I did it, but what stuck with me were the life-lessons I was given, lessons that I never received any other way in my life. Lessons that to do this day effect and shape me in how I am.

When you talk about learning life-lessons, the only way you do that is by living or experiencing them.

Seeing and doing is reality.

It gave me an appreciation for life, and showed how to not take it for granted. As a firefighter you see it up close all the time. Many times, that split-second accident costs someone their life. There is no minimum age to die. Sadly, I pulled people of all ages out of deadly car wrecks and fires. Appreciate the life you have, and that God has given you.

It showed me to appreciate the simple things. A warm house in winter really means a lot when you've just come home from an overnight house fire in the middle of January in Wisconsin, where the family lost everything. Four kids now have no clothes and no toys. Put yourself in their shoes for a day and you'll be thankful for the shoes you have.

It made me appreciate and cherish lifelong friends. Friendships I made with other firefighters live on to this day. They're like brothers/sisters. Real lifelong friends should be viewed this way. When you die, who will be at your funeral? These are the people you should care most about and call from time to time. If you need something, they're there. People like this don't come into your life every day. For some, these types of people never come to the surface. They never find them. So, if you have them, cherish them. Tell them you love them.

My time on the fire department showed me to never assume you'll do something forever.

It taught me to live and appreciate the here and now.

Looking back, those five firefighting years were a blur. Before I knew it, I was no longer on the department. I wish I would have taken a step back at times and enjoyed it a little bit more. The camaraderie and fun we had will never happen again. Guys died, moved on, and very few are left on the department to this day. I go back from time to time to talk to the guys who now run the trucks I did. But the one thing that does live on in life, are the memories.

Remember to ask yourself, how you want to be remembered. Smile and say thank you.

Say I love you and don't forget to live life.

My time as a firefighter showed me the aspects of life that many never see. How short life can really be. How fast tragedy can strike. How quickly it can all end.

It changes your views on things that you thought were the most important to not be as important. You align your priorities according to what really matters in your life.

From that vantage point it changed how I viewed money. It made me become a better spouse, father, business owner, and employer. Things that I stressed and worried about, it turns out, are so minor in the grand scheme of things that I worried and stressed less.

Days that I think are bad or tough will bring back memories from a fire or accident where an individual and their family actually had it tough. What I'm viewing as a tough day, is nothing compared to their tough days. I've seen them up close. It's tough and heartbreaking, but it shows that life is all about your perspective.

Health, family, happiness, spending time with those you want to spend time with, is what matters most. Aiming for your dreams and going after goals rather than saying "I'll get to that someday" changed. Live in the now and go after it today. Don't waste time on the unimportant. Don't stress or worry about the small stuff. Things can always be worse, so continue working to make them the best you can.

2
Keep Life In Perspective

Before this book digs deep into business and becoming successful, please keep in mind: live life.

There will come a time that you get tired of chasing the almighty dollar. The preverbal goalpost will stop moving. You must be able to enjoy your successes, otherwise you'll no longer recognize or appreciate them. No matter how well you do or how much money you make, it will not matter.

I know many people who wish they would have done this earlier in life. A lot of people do not realize this until it's too late. It is the most draining marathon you will ever run. Imagine running that race every day of your life, 24/7/365. There are never enough hours in the day. There is never enough money to be made. Time off and time with family too often turn into "I don't have time for that."

So please, if you don't get anything else out of this book, slow down, look at your life and ask yourself: How are you living? Would those who love you most be happy with your life?
Would they smile or shake their head at you?

What is Wealth?

For most of my life I have battled the constant pursuit

of more. Regardless of what I've achieved, or what level of success I've had, I could never seem to reach any state of satisfaction. There was always more to achieve, or a new success to reach. It turned out contentment had become an ever-moving goalpost.

We live in a near constant state of discontentment. We always want more money, a bigger house, another house, more clothing, more toys, more clients, more followers, etc. No matter how much we achieve, more always exists. There is always another mountain to climb, or another box to check. The societal pressures keep you longing for more and more.

Here is a section from the book *Essentialism* by Greg McKeown that I often look to for a proper perspective:

"What if society stopped telling us to buy more stuff and instead allowed us to create more space to breathe and think? What if society encouraged us to reject what has been accurately described as doing things we detest, to buy things we don't need, with money we don't have, to impress people we don't like?

"What if we stopped being oversold the value of having more and being undersold the value of having less?

"What if we stopped celebrating being busy as a measurement of importance? What if instead we celebrated how much time we had spent listening, pondering, meditating, and enjoying time with the most important people in our lives?

"What if the whole world shifted from the undisciplined pursuit of more to the disciplined pursuit of less…only better?"

Just as the definition of wealth can be different from

person to person, so can the definition of success. My view of success will be different than yours. What truly matters is how you view success.

If one is wealthy in money, he's envious of another's time. If one is wealthy in time, he's envious of another's money. We can be so envious of what another has.

We chase more money, more fame, and more power. We look around and compare ourselves to our friends, neighbors, co-workers and even people we don't know. The constant pursuit of more never slows down. Everything passes us by with our constant thirst for more. The finish line doesn't exist. How much is enough? When does happiness and contentment set in?

Choose to play your own game, then you can slow or even stop your ever-moving goalpost and decide for yourself what success, enough, and wealth are. It's all about your perspective.

Put Yourself In Their Shoes

Every day we make hundreds of decisions. Many are made without even giving a thought to them. It's the decisions that we wrestle with and think about that we remember.

The hardest decisions we make are usually those that will most impact others. If you own a business or are in a career where you make decisions for others, you know what I mean.

It's normal to question if you're making the right decisions. Second guessing is a part of the daily thought process, but it's your decision, and once you make it, you have to live with it.

So, how do we become better decision makers? How do we satisfy our clients? How do we make better decisions for our businesses? How do we become better at leading our teams? Navigate important decisions by applying the following thought process and old adage: Put yourself in their shoes.

It sounds too simple, and it really is, but it's too often overlooked. If you're making decisions that affect and motivate, or trying to satisfy others, this should be one of the first things you consider.

If you own a business and are trying to motivate your teammates in the form of bonuses or incentives, put yourself in their shoes: What kind of bonus or incentive would motivate you? Maybe you would like to be asked and given the option to pick a certain bonus or incentive?

If you're trying to determine whether you should contact your clients ahead of time about a procedure or pricing change coming at your business, put yourself in their shoes: Would you want to be notified about this? What type of options would you want to be offered? What kind of improvement or options would you like to see added as a client of your company or user of your product?

If you're thinking of making major changes to your business, put yourself in their shoes: How would this change affect your clients view on your business? What impact would this have on your employees? If you are a customer of your business and this change was made, how would you react? How would you feel? Would you shop your business to a competitor?

If you want to send a thank you gift to employees, centers of influence, or clients, put yourself in their shoes: What would you want to receive as a gift? What is a gift that would be useful or make a lasting impression on you?

Using this thought process brings empathy to the forefront. You'll stop yourself from making costly errors by making this a part of your checklist when making decisions. The more important the decision, the more you look at the consequences and effects of your decision by putting yourself in someone else's shoes. It matters and goes a long way in building trust, establishing relationships and resolving situations.

As I look back at many of the best decisions I've made, I had put myself in that particular team member's or client's shoes. How would I feel? How would I want to be thanked, incentivized, told that I need to do better, and so on.

Your decision affects others, whether it be positive or negative. They're no different than you, still another human being. They breathe the same air and put their pants on one leg at a time like you.

If you want to make smarter decisions, better understand people, be a better leader, friend, parent, and spouse, step out of your shoes once in a while and put yourself in theirs for a moment.

Treat Others How You Want To Be Treated

Putting yourself in someone else's shoes isn't only limited to friends or family. This does not just go for your employees or clients; this should be done with everyone that you ever encounter. It's always easy to view things from your point of view, but try to look at things with another perspective.

Something that I have always tried to live by, is treating everyone the same. In insurance we deal with people of all different income levels and social statuses. When everyone needs your product, you get a wide array of clients.

During my first year in business, I recall a Wednesday afternoon in August. I received an email from a CEO of a Fortune 500 company. He wanted insurance quotes on his auto, home, boats, and umbrella insurance.

Like any other prospective client, I asked the same questions. Knowing his name and who he was, I was a little more thorough in the information I had to gather as we were talking about some high value items.

Towards the end of the call, I got the opportunity to ask some questions about his work and business career. I knew his time was limited, but he was gracious with me and answered them. I provided him quotes, but due to some underwriting guidelines we were unable to help him.

Later that day we had a lady contact us for an auto insurance quote. As we were quoting her, we brought up the discount of adding home or renter's insurance as it would reduce the cost on her auto insurance.

She proceeded to inform me that she didn't own or rent. I said, do you still live at home with your parents? She replied no. I had to ask, what was her living situation? I could tell by the silence on the other end of the line it was not going to be a normal response. She said she lived out of her car and was homeless.

Now, coming from a very small town of 1,200 people, I'd never come across someone that was homeless. For a moment I didn't know what to say.

As I quickly gathered my thoughts, I proceeded to discuss just her auto insurance. The next day she came into the office, and we insured her vehicle. She was very proud to be able to insure her vehicle and pay for her first month, because she knew that having auto insurance is state law and didn't want to be fined. She stated that she was never able to afford auto insurance until now.

That weekend as I sat in my apartment, I thought back to these two completely different people; one, very blessed and successful, the other, struggling to make ends meet. Where did their paths go in such drastically opposite directions?

I would have been happy to help both out that day. Only the homeless women became a client, but that interaction stuck with me. So often I take for granted the very simple things in life.

Some are just looking for ways to survive and make it day to day. We don't have to look too far to be appreciative for things that we have and the blessed lives we live. Not everyone is as fortunate.

I am happy to say that a few months later we got another call back from the homeless woman and she was no longer homeless. Now she was able to rent an apartment and she remembered me asking about the discount on the auto insurance and said she wanted to get that discount. But she also wanted to get renters insurance to be sure the bed and couch she got would be covered.

To this day she has her auto and renters insurance with my agency. She has since also added life insurance. Don't forget to appreciate the little things in life.

Don't Prejudge Anyone

Have you ever heard the phrase "always make a good first impression"? What do you do when someone doesn't make a good first impression on you? You may have heard the stories of people, badly dressed with disheveled hair and dirty shoes, being millionaires and becoming the best clients.

Often in sales we have the vision of the perfect client. They're well dressed, driving a high-end luxury car. Things that tell you he likes the finer things in life and will have the money to buy your most expensive product. Those identifiable clients can be easy.

But what about everyone else? Seeing what they drive or how they dress might be a front.

Could that person be deeply in debt and living off credit? Absolutely, he could. You will not know until you make your presentation or get the sale.

Could that next person that comes through the door be dressed like an average joe—or even below-average joe—and possess millions of dollars in his bank account? Of course, he could.

What we've found in our observations of clients over our years of research is that the first impressions really do not tell us much at all. Most of the time they tell us nothing. When comparing the first impressions and the facts, we discovered that the first impressions were usually wrong.

After realizing this, we decided to adapt all our sales presentation and pitches to be the same regardless of how we may have pre-classified the client. We stopped trying to adapt presentations to how much money we perceived they had or trying to determine what they could afford. We treat every client the same.

If someone wanted to talk about life insurance, we presented the same type of plans to a single mom with kids and to a financially secure large business owner. Now, the amount of coverage and pricing was different, but it was the same general discussion. We asked the same exploratory questions on what their objectives were. The presentation and design of the programs were the same. How much they wanted to contribute or could afford varied however.

Many times, this approach led to someone who could have been classified during a first impression assessment as a non-preferred prospective client being one of our best clients.

They bought more from us because they had a different mindset and set of priorities.

They may view care for their family as paramount on their financial program. What if that single mother passed away prematurely? She'd want to leave her kids with enough money that they are financially stable for their entire life. She'd want their college fully paid for. She's leaving a legacy for her family long after she is gone.

A wealthy business owner may have different priorities. Maybe his large payments for other things are higher on his priority list. Therefore, the money he wants to allocate for his life insurance program is very little.

You can save the brain power and time trying to prejudge someone on their outer appearances. You really don't know what makes them tick inside. Everyone has different priorities, incomes, beliefs, and buying triggers.

3

One Team, One Goal

Talk with any successful business owner or any company executive and a constant answer to what makes their company so successful will be their employees. It was the same when I was a firefighter. We had to be a strong team or we'd have major problems and people would get hurt. Who you're working with makes all the difference. The team that you surround yourself with will be one of the single most important aspects of your business. So how do you get rockstar teammates? This could probably be an entire book on its own, but I will highlight what has worked for me.

You spend so much time at work and with your team. Just to make it clear, I refer to my employees and office staff as my team. We are all working together towards the same goals. To me, that is a team and that is how we operate and identify ourselves.

That might be the first thing you have to change if you own a business with employees.

Adjust that mindset—not just your own—the whole team's. If they do not buy into the team concept, then it's time to make some changes with your people and find people who are team players.

What do sports teams do when you hear of a player becoming a distraction or cancer to the team, or not buying into the system? They trade or release them.

You must run your business the same way. Sports teams draft players specific to their systems. Who will fit your team and system the best? You must hire that way.

In many cases you'll spend as much time with them in a week as you do your family. So, you better hire good ones!

Finding people can be challenging or easy. It's easy when you have an opening come up and you have a list of names. It's hard when you need to hire someone, and you don't have any names or people to talk with. Always have a list of people you would like to hire if you have an opening. Maybe currently you can't afford someone, but soon that could change. Always keep an updated and current list of names.

I keep an active list of people to hire. Whenever I come across someone that I'd like to talk to or consider, I put their name down.

If you have a good customer service experience with someone, make a note of it. It might be someone worth interviewing who could fit your team.

I got the most names from banks and coffee shops. Many may not work out, but if you get one teammate that stays with you twenty years it's worth a lot to you and your business.

Finding Teammates

So how do you find people to be a part of your team or company? Where are they? How do you find that teammate who stays with you twenty years? Where do you begin to find the potential family-like employees?

Look around you. You want others who would be

focused on helping build your business; people who are engaging, motivated, and create memorable experiences. They should be on your team. Stop looking so hard and look at who's around you.

Think about who you come across in a day.

Where do you go each day, week, or month? The bank, grocery store, coffee shops, restaurants, retail stores, gym and so on. Others you see or meet at sporting events, social gatherings and school activities.

Now look for the WOW experiences. Who gives them? Are there people who leave a meaningful impact on you during a sales or service related experience, in person or over the phone? Are they people who leave you saying:

- "I enjoyed working with them, I'll do business with them again."
- "They made that easy."
- "They seem very nice."
- "What a great problem solver."
- "I wish they worked for me, or with me."

Target these people! If you come across people that you say this about and you aren't hiring at the moment, or have an opening, be sure you add their information in a "people to hire" file.

This gives you the names of people to add to your team or business at any time. Maintain contact with them. Maybe every few months you make a point to see them. You have rapport, you know where they are, and then, when the time is right, you're able to make it work.

What about your current team? What do you have in place for your current team to find talent to bring to your company? People like to work with friends. If anyone knows the abilities of a person and what traits they would bring to your company, wouldn't their close friend be the perfect person to give insight? This also has your team keeping an eye out for WOW experiences in every person they come across in their daily life. Including your teammates in this process shows the value you place in them and they'll see that.

Giving a bonus if you hire someone your teammates refer makes them think about working with their friends. Look at the lifetime value of a hire! It's worth making it a worthwhile bonus. Make it a large bonus! It motivates and it'll always be in the back of their mind.

Job postings are overrated. Job postings only appeal to people who are out looking for a job. How do you appeal to people who are high performers in their current job and aren't scouring job posting sites or replying to a billboard advertising a certain hourly wage? If someone is replying to your hourly wage advertisement on a billboard, they're basing their decision solely on the price per hour your company is offering. If you advertise and make it about an hourly wage, that's what your prospective teammate will be solely focused on. The company offering the most money doesn't always win.

What about friends? Much of the consensus has always been don't hire friends, or be friends with employees. I've always had a different view and often refer to the story of PayPal and the PayPal Mafia. Here is a quote from an article in TechRepublic on hiring friends and friendship by PayPal:

"'When we started PayPal, I remember one of the

early conversations I had with Max [Levchin] was that I wanted to build a company where everybody would be really great friends and, no matter what happened with the company, the friendships would survive,' former PayPal CEO Peter Thiel said. 'In some ways that was very utopian. We didn't only hire our friends, but we did hire people that we thought we could become really good friends with.'

"Many of those friendships began at Stanford. Keith Rabois, David O. Sacks, Reid Hoffman, and Ken Howery all attended Stanford around the same time and most were subsequently recruited by Thiel to work for PayPal. Max Levchin recruited some developers and former classmates from the University of Illinois at Urbana-Champaign as well.

"What's unique is that the majority of the early PayPal employees, and the PayPal Mafia in general, were all recruited through a friendship network and not by a headhunter. Sacks said that these people were 'cut from the same cloth.' This, he said, explained how they all had such a strong entrepreneurial focus to begin with."

If that was the mindset and one of the founding principles for the greatest collection of entrepreneurial talent of all-time, it should be good enough for every small and large business.

Hire the person, not for the role. Quit waiting and looking only for people who check all the boxes in what you want for a specific role. In a different hiring environment this was possible. Now it isn't. Stop being so picky. There is always a place for people who are honest, driven, loyal, hard-working, and so on. This may be friends or close acquaintances. Many of these attributes are not trainable or coachable. They're natural human attributes that people possess.

The right people are eager to learn and be trained. If you only hire on crossing every "t" and dotting every "i" on job descriptions, work history, education, and on and on, you're going to continue to struggle finding people.

Don't make the process of finding teammates so hard. Remember to look at the people around you.

Don't Hire Employees

When firefighters arrive on the scene, one of the responsibilities is to set a perimeter.

Cones, flashing lights, and lots of orange to grab everyone's attention. This protects the firefighters during the rescue, but it also tells anyone who would be passing through to slow down, take caution, and avoid going down that road.

Two of the warning lights for me when I'm hiring new teammates are job switchers and the long-time unemployed. Both of these tell me, "Slow Down! Don't go down that road!"

Switching jobs often is the very first thing that will get someone's resume tossed. It's the clearest indication that you have of someone's past in a work environment. If someone is a job jumper, then I don't want them to be part of my team. That screams "NO" to me. They are not career minded, but, more importantly, they are not team minded.

Teams need to be built over time, so trust can be built. Someone who's unwilling to stick with it through the hard times will often be complainers even during

23

the good times. I know that the average person changes jobs ten to fifteen times in their working life, but I'm not looking for average. I'm looking for the best.

Work history is very important and finding out why they left their recent jobs needs to be asked. Why are they looking to change jobs now? Review the work history and ask a lot of questions. It's the most important thing on a resume.

Don't shy away from the tough questions and if you do not feel comfortable, move on. If you hire someone that doesn't work out you'll have wasted a lot of time, resources, and money. Be slow to hire and quick to fire are words to live by if you are an employer.

Now, there are many reasons for someone being away from the job market. They may have been a stay-at-home mother or had a recent medical condition. There are major personal events and societal events that can take people out of the market. For many, I will talk with them, but if they have just been "looking" or "waiting," I don't want any part of them.

It tells me they are lacking a work ethic and motivation. The longer you go without work the weaker and weaker your work ethic becomes. You lose that drive and itch. Sure, it may come back, but I'm not going to gamble and risk it.

I want someone who is sharp, competitive, and on top of their game. I can cite far too many examples where long-time unemployed hires do not work out. Tread very carefully with this group.

I need people on my team that will work hard and support each other well. I need them to stick with it and work through the difficult times. When people talk to me about hiring, I always use the word teammate. Maybe you've noticed. I don't like the word employee.

Employees are individuals. Employees "just work here." Teammates are a part of something bigger. Teammates understand that they and everyone else contribute to make things better, better for everyone. Hire teammates, not employees.

Clear Communication

Once you have identified a good candidate or someone you would like to hire, set specific duties and responsibilities with them. Review them one by one and ask if that's what they like doing or would be comfortable doing. Be open and honest about it. Address it up front so you are on the same page.

Then, if they do get hired, you're hitting the ground running and they know what to prepare for. Go over examples and how things will be done. See if they have questions, ask if that is comfortable to them. It sets a vision so that they can be sure it will be a position and company that they will enjoy working with. Set the expectations and review job duties before you get into offering and accepting a candidate.

I go over the entire process and even then, will have them do an interview with my two highest ranking teammates. I will also introduce them to the entire team. First impressions are usually good indicators and the more input and information I can get from my team on someone the better, more informed decision I can make. Allow your teammates to help you and listen to what they say. Just because you are the boss doesn't mean you're always right. You don't have to do it all alone.

Making Your Employees Like Family

Today, it's very hard to find long term employees. I have been very fortunate that so far in my years in business I have only lost a couple teammates.

As my team grew, I had to find teammates, interview, and hire them. I did not have an HR firm or career employment agency send people to me. It was up to me to find and hire who I thought would best fit my team. Thankfully, the decisions I made were the right ones. Let's examine some of the main qualities I looked for and red flags that jump out to me:

Personality. Hopefully, you know what type of a personality you are as well as the others that work with you. If you have a laid-back group of easy going, genuinely nice people, then that is what you continue hiring.

My team has always been a group whose personalities are all very similar. I have interviewed very high-strung people with very strong personalities. Although they were very nice people with great resumes, I knew they weren't going to fit my team.

Don't try to fit a square peg in a round hole is how I've always viewed it. Stick with what works.

Teamwork. Have they been a part of a team? Do they work in a team or group setting now where they strive with others for a common goal? Some have that competitive edge to them and that comes through activities where they compete to be the best.

Personally, I hate losing and when talking to prospective hires you can tell what someone's competitive nature is. Ask open ended questions about their past where they have experienced teamwork, or competitive activities. If they're already working in your industry or business type, ask what their production and performance has been.

Honesty. Probably the single hardest thing to search out is someone's honesty level. Two things that I've done to try and seek this out the best I can is to talk to their references or mutual friends, if you have them.

The other is to ask questions about how they would handle certain situations. The key indicator is not so much what they say, it's how long it takes them to answer and how much thought they must give. It should be instinctive, like the snap of a finger, for a genuinely honest person with high integrity.

Holding Your Team Accountable

When I was a firefighter I worked as a part of a team to help people during stressful and life or death situations. It was imperative that everyone knew their role to achieve our goal. You worked as a team where everyone knew what they had to do.

How was someone's role determined? Their role was made to fit their strengths. The best teams find people's strengths and how to best utilize those strengths within their team. Then they're held accountable for that role. This ensures everyone is in their best position possible while working towards a goal as one tight-knit team.

If you have employees or are starting to realize you need employees, you have come to understand that you can't run a successful, growing business all by yourself. It's almost impossible.

Your team needs to know what your business's goals are. What are your goals for the year? Where do you want your business to be in five years? Do you plan on expanding? If so, when? The better question may be, do you know the answers to these questions? If you don't, how can you share these goals with your team?

Each member of your team should know what role and responsibility they play in attaining these goals. All great teams are made up of teammates that know what their roles are.

Having goals and establishing how each person contributes to achieving them shows what their accountability is. View it as everyone pushing something together. If there are some that don't buy in and aren't pushing, they may as well be pushing against the rest of you. They need to be accountable for what is expected of them. By each working towards their individual part allows the entire team and company to reach their goals.

The sales team knows how many sales they need to make. The customer service team knows what their retention and churn rate must be.

All these goals should be shared with your team, but first you need to know the goals and numbers that you want your business to reach.

Rewarding Your Teammates

With setting goals and expectations for your team you must be ready to align your compensation to incentivize them to reach those goals. When your business is making money and thriving, so should your teammates. Reward them and don't be a cheapskate.

If you have worked as an employee, you know what it's like to be on the other side of that desk. Give yearly raises. Have annual compensation reviews. Talk openly and freely about the expectations that you have. Many times employers make the mistake of not properly laying out the expectations for an employee.

Make their job duties and responsibilities clear. In our agency I have a workflow chart. It lists the various jobs and responsibilities, and each team member knows what they are responsible for doing.

Another important duty when having employees is being in tune with what others in their position are making within the industry. How are they being compensated? I knew a long-time business owner that was having a hard time keeping his current staff and being able to hire new people.

After we spoke about it, the problem was very clear. He didn't keep up with the pay grade for that role. When two of his current employees poked around at other jobs, they realized that they were severely under compensated for the duties and roles they had.

Had that business owner been keeping up with the local industry trends and pay scales he may have avoided the need to hire and train the three new people it took to replace those two. A loss of time and money.

What do you do to compensate your teammates? It starts with knowing what other companies are paying their top people. You want to make sure, if you have some of the best teammates, that they're compensated properly. Put yourself in their shoes. What would you want?

The first and most obvious is money. Our team's

salespeople are compensated by salary or hourly and commissions or bonuses based upon how much they sell. The sales are where they make the majority of their money. The triggers at each level are good chunks of money. You must make the next level well worth it.

A simple way to view this is the more they sell, the more money they're ultimately making your business. Do not be frugal with your salespeople. If they're working hard and bringing in good business, then they should be rewarded.

Benefits have become one of the most sought-after compensations. Health insurance and retirement are things that must be discussed. Sometimes you will have to adapt your benefits if you need to keep a teammate or your entire team. Benefits, many times, are just as important to people as their salary. A retirement, stock options, or profit-sharing plan is a great perk that as a business owner you need to consider providing.

I've always allowed my team to work their own schedule. If they want to leave early or have something that requires them to come in a bit later, that's fine with me. They know that it's up to them to make up their time.

I don't make them punch a time clock. I rely on and trust that they will work the amount of time that they are expected to. Putting the trust factor on them, I believe, makes them appreciate how trusting I am in them.

In all my years, I've never had a teammate take advantage of this. They're aware of their vacation days, how many hours they're expected to work or how much business they're expected to write. Maybe I have special teammates, actually, I know I do. Trust and appreciation is a two way street. Be sure you're showing yours.

Team Meetings

The best place to share our goals and have the best discussion about improving and becoming a world class team is in team meetings.

We have monthly meetings for both my sales and service team within my insurance agency. I have come to realize that this was one of the most important things that I started after being in business a few years. This allows the team to be in a controlled meeting setting, rather than trying to talk while the phones are ringing and people are coming into the office.

We have the meetings first thing in the morning and put a note on the door stating "meeting in progress."

This is the perfect time to discuss changes being made or needing to be made. It allows for the discussion of challenges or issues amongst the team. It lets us all brainstorm problem solving and improvement strategies.

When I'm pondering a new idea or change, I bring it up in the meeting so we can all have input. It's a roundtable brainstorming discussion. It's a much better use of our time versus going to everyone individually.

Our goals and where we are currently in pursuing them are discussed. If we are lacking or need improvement, this is the platform to bring it up. It can be worked at and discussed as a team. If we're behind on a certain goal everyone knows and they know what I expect us to do about it.

Sometimes there are hard conversations and topics that need to be discussed, but as the owner and leader you must do it. I have found it's much easier to do this when talking to the team together. Then as a team we can come up with new ideas and strategies to get where we want to be.

Your Secret Team

You're not able to do everything yourself. You're going to need help along the way. That does not just mean your employees. You need to surround yourself with a team of, what I like to call, advisors. They are my experts on all things accounting and legal. These are not areas where I'm an expert. That is not my job.

If I wanted to be an attorney and know the legality of business or wanted to be an expert on the tax code, I would have become a lawyer or accountant. Instead, I rely on the advice of the best accountant and lawyer that I can find.

Regularly scheduled meetings with my accountant and lawyer are just as important as the meetings that I conduct with my sales and service teams. We discuss the financial and legal aspects of my business. The behind the scenes stuff is integral and I like to view it as the control or boiler room of a business.

Attorneys. Yes, I know they've got a bad reputation. But when you're in business you better get used to dealing with them. The legal end of your business is a very overlooked aspect. Problems with employees, advertising, lawsuits, and general legal counsel all go through my attorneys. When creating advertising or doing things that can expose my business, I consult my attorney. Yes, they're costly but their advice could save you thousands and even millions of dollars.

To find a law firm of attorneys to represent and work with me and my business, I asked other medium-to-large sized businesses, not so much in the insurance industry, but companies in my area. I did come to find that many had their own in-house law team. But the others that didn't, used local firms and gave me some great referrals.

The firm I chose is one that works with multiple types of businesses and different levels of industries. My thinking was the more exposure they have to general business counsel, the better.

I will meet with them when I have a project or a few things to discuss. The advice and tips they give back to me are immensely helpful and well worth the extra money. They give you not what you'd like to hear, but keep it real and relay the law to you in common English. Trust me, it will help you understand why you can't do this or that. Find a well-regarded firm that specializes in small-to-medium sized businesses. It could end up saving you millions or even your business.

Accountants. Numbers, numbers, and more numbers. Ah, the life of an accountant. Sounds fun, doesn't it? Or would you prefer dealing with the IRS tax code every day.

It's what might be the single most important outside counsel any business has. If you own a business, you probably already know this. Trust me when I tell you that if you don't have a good accountant and your bookkeeping isn't in line you will not be in business very long.

A common phrase you will hear about an accountant is, "A good accountant can save you a ton of money." On the flip side you'll hear "A bad accountant can cost you a lot of money." A good accountant knows your business and how it operates.

When I was starting my business, I knew I needed to find the best accountant I could. I figured the insurance business is complex, so I should find an accountant that knows the insurance business.

Well, how do I do that? They don't exactly advertise as accountants specializing in insurance agencies. I asked others that owned long time successful insurance agencies. To my surprise a couple of them used the same firm and same specific accountant.

To this day I still use the same accountant. We meet at the end of every quarter. I cannot emphasize how important my relationship is with my accountant. We monitor where all the financials are, current payroll, whether we are ok to expand and, if so, when, how many new employees we can comfortably onboard. He knows the health of my business as much as I do. This allows me the time to work on my business and on the things that grow the company.

If you speak with other successful business owners, they will also explain the importance of a good accountant. Some may tell you their horror stories. Others may jump to tell you about how good theirs is. My stories are happy and very complimentary. Don't wait, and don't try to skimp when hiring the best you can find. The relationship you develop, and the time and money they will save you over your working years, is well worth it.

Banker. When you're ready to expand or need

money to help your business grow, where do you go? The bank.

Having an established relationship with a banker is important. They're a partner in trying to grow your business. If there is a level of trust on both sides that makes the unknowns of loans, banks, and expanding a business less daunting.

Many times they have examples or ideas that can help in your business's growth. The perspective they have is interesting because business lenders deal with all kinds of businesses in all different industries.

Over the years I have learned a lot from my bankers. Some on the business side but also on the personal side of things. There are different ways of doing things for your business banking as well as your personal banking.

This is another area where most people aren't experts. Rely on the ones who are experts. Use their advice and knowledge to your advantage and to help you improve your business and personal finances.

4

Familiarity And Trust

People do business with people they know and trust. Companies do business with companies they know and trust. Familiarity and trust is what people want. That is what people gravitate toward.

Starting out, my team was my one assistant Patricia and I. She handled the servicing and I handled the sales. Her expertise was the service side and the technical behind-the-scenes stuff.

My goal was to find new clients to grow our agency.

As we continued to grow over the years, we added team members. When I added team members, I would identify them as being a service-oriented person or possessing more of a sales mindset. If I needed sales help, I'd look for people that would thrive in that role.

I tried a few things, but found the most success in hiring people for service, and, through working with them, identifying if they were cut out for the sales team. I found some of my best salespeople that way.

Service oriented people want to build familiarity and trust. Many salespeople just want to get to the next sell. It's a one-and-done mentality and I think our society is sick of it. We don't trust salespeople.

That's one of the reasons many don't want to work in sales. It's not for everybody, but my teammates could try it and, if they didn't find success, they could always return to service. The task, then, is finding teammates who provide a great service experience.

They aren't that hard to find. It happens at places you go. You just need to be on the lookout. Great people fit on your team. If someone gives you a wow experience, they should be on your team. Get their name or card, and ask if you can speak with them sometime. You are familiar with them and they have your trust, they could probably do the same for your team.

I asked the long, tenured clients of my company why they stuck with us and their responses were: "I know what to expect," "I trust you," "You have taken care of me in the past," "I am familiar with everyone here," and "I've known you as long as you've been here."

What do these answers all come back to? What is the common denominator? They are all based on familiarity and trust. So, how do you build familiarity and trust? I'll share with you next what we've done.

Client Focused Relationship Model

My team and I wanted to take our service to another level with our clients. The concept was separating our service and sales teams. This allowed us to provide more personalized service to our existing clients and a more specialized approach for our prospective clients.

My service team is broken into three parts. The Customer Service Reps are responsible for handling the front desk, greeting and welcoming clients, taking care of the phone calls by answering questions, and handling changes with client accounts.

For Account Managers, the alphabet was split up.

They were taking the service-related functions that an agent would usually focus on. They would handle the underwriting duties, writing new policies and working with clients, reviewing their current policies.

The Marketing and Retention Specialist is responsible for setting up our marketing programs and ideas. Their focus is on driving business to our agency through marketing initiatives. They also work on retention programs and ideas to improve client satisfaction with our agency.

My sales team is made up of two parts. Sales Branch Managers are responsible for making sure our sales goals are being obtained by our team. They help the sales reps with questions they have and work with them on ways to write more business. They'll also train the new sales reps.

Sales Reps make up the second part of the sales team. They spend their days working with people by creating relationships and making sales to turn people into clients. They bring new families to the agency that we want to work with.

Our team members were then able to focus on what they're best at. What they enjoy doing is how we helped steer who fit in what roles best. We weren't trying to fit round pegs in square holes anymore. Happy team and happy clients. It's a great recipe.

This client-focused, relationship-building model started to really work wonders. Instead of every client asking for me, they got used to working with their account manager, or the same person who had answered the phone. Familiarity and trust really came full circle.

This setup also allows for a business owner to not

need to go into the office every day. I was able to step back and get out of the way. You can work on your business, not just in it.

Things will run without me. It is not reliant on me and it's definitely not reliant on me working 60-70 hours a week.

Delegating and replacing myself with my teammates allows for me to focus on what I want to do. If I want to work on something creative, say this book, I can. Create your freedom. Create your life.

This model allows you to manage and oversee instead of doing everything yourself. Because of it, we didn't just maintain our high levels of retention and client satisfaction, we pushed them to our all-time agency highs.

What about our agency production? Well, we became one of the highest producing agencies in the country. We took another leap in our growth. This also put us on the path to breaking a 90-year company sales record for life insurance.

5

Client Relationships

Taking care of your existing clients is often overlooked. We take them for granted. Every business does. Most are just stable and solid customers. They're repeat buyers of your products and services. They make their payments on time and don't have issues. So often in our business we don't hear from them.

For many years I took them for granted. My team was always focused on getting new clients. We were not spending enough time and energy on taking care of our already satisfied clients.

What really woke me up was reading, *No B.S. Marketing to the Affluent*, by Dan S. Kennedy. There was a line that stuck with me, "When your clients go out to dinner with their friends, do they brag about you? If the answer is no, then you've got work to do."

At the time I read that, the answer for most of my clients would have been no.

That was going to change. In our industry the competition is fierce. Insurance commercials and competitors are lurking at every turn. It was time to firm up our relationships with our clients.

There was a day about a week after reading this book where I had two longtime clients leave for another company. The reasons they gave were both the same. "I have not heard from you or your staff in years." I couldn't believe that so I took a look at their accounts. They were right! Somehow they'd fallen through the cracks of all the programs we were doing to reach out.

If it happened to them, I'm sure there are others. We were going to test and implement programs that would make sure we connect with clients multiple times a year. We work so hard to get new clients, we need to work even harder to prove our value to current clients who want to continue working with us.

We tested and perfected programs for existing clients. The programs made a tremendous improvement to our retention and relationships with our clients. We grew our retention rates to an all-time high. These are the five programs that we use and have in place today.

- Welcome Program
- Newsletter
- Review Program
- Referrals and Centers of Influence
- WOW Gift Program

Welcome Program

When you begin in business your focus is on bringing in new business by making sales. You want to bring in as many new clients as possible. Your mindset is to grow as fast as you can.

Something that often gets overlooked, however, is the importance of keeping people who are already clients of your business.

If you bring in two new client accounts to your business but lose two client accounts, you've gone nowhere. You've not grown. All that work and you end the day where you began. Client retention is just as important as getting new clients.

It's a balancing act. The sooner you realize that both carry an equal amount of weight, the faster your business will grow.

Unfortunately, it took me longer than I want to admit to completely realize this. Our data told us that we were weak in our newer client retention. Our new clients with a tenure under three years was unacceptable. In fact, it down right stunk!

That was when my team and I put together a New Client Welcome Program. We wanted to improve our newer client retention and work on ways to get clients to the five year mark with our firm. Our data showed that if clients could make it to five years, the retention rate spiked and hardly anyone left us.

It took some time but years later our client household retention is now at almost 97% for families under three years of tenure with our firm. Families with five years tenure and above stand at an almost 99% retention rate.

For an insurance firm, which is within a very competitive industry that traditionally sees a lot of turnover with clients moving among companies, I'm very proud of the numbers my team has accomplished.

What did we change? Our focus was on the new families we brought on as clients. We changed it by implementing our New Client Welcome Program. This program was in addition to the newsletter that we developed which goes out to all our clients quarterly. I'll share more about the newsletter next.

Once a new family joins our firm as a client, the following month we start to implement our program.

Here is what our three-part New Client Welcome Program entails.

The first part is a welcome folder. Why send a welcome folder when you can just send an email? Everything is paperless and online now. Communication is done by companies through email and apps now. This is precisely why we send one. It's unexpected and different. They're going to look and read through what's in the folder. Think about what you do when you receive something that's unexpected through the mail?

We've found that it both serves a purpose and makes an impact. As we've met with clients over the years, it's not uncommon for most of them to bring that folder to their meetings with us. They still use and reference it.

What goes into the folder depends on your business. What do you want to tell them?

What do they need to know? What should they expect as a client of your company? We created a guide for them. This is a colored pamphlet which presents our team's pictures and explains our firm, who does what and what's to be expected, what they should do when they need a certain thing done, and gives ways to contact us and our various departments.

We also include a referral card notifying them about our referral program. To create upsell opportunities you could include information on products or services that they don't have with you. There may be giveaway items that would be helpful or meaningful to them. You could include some form of a thank you card. Include things that you'd find beneficial. Create your folder and then constantly be updating and improving upon it.

The second part of our New Client Welcome Program is a welcome gift. Once a family is a client with our firm for two years we send them a welcome gift. Our welcome gift that has had the best success is a custom engraved cutting board and a gas card. Along with this gift, we include a letter thanking them for their continued business and trust. It also asks if they have any questions or need anything from us.

The idea behind this is to give them something of use. Something they would keep and even use frequently. It's meant to reinforce that we value them and their business with our firm.

The third part is a face-to-face meeting. After being with our firm for three years we make a point to reach out to clients by email and phone to schedule an appointment. We'll continue contacting them until we hear back to set up a time. Our goal is meeting in person. We may meet at one of our offices or their home, or we'll take them to coffee, meet for lunch, or take lunch to them. There are many unique and different ways to meet with your clients.

The idea behind this appointment isn't to upsell anything. It's just to talk with them. To see if they need anything, and check if there is anything we could improve on or do better for them. We want to thank them for their business and reinstill their importance to our firm. This appointment is just about having a nice casual conversation. It usually entails very little talk about their actual business with us.

In any business no matter what product or service you're selling, it's all based upon relationships and trust. Just because someone becomes a client doesn't mean your work is done. The most important part is just beginning.

The competition for business is fierce. It always has and always will be. How do you stand out and do things differently than your competitors? What type of a relationship do you have with your clients? Are you working to deepen those relationships? Continue growing trust by deepening your relationships.

Newsletter

One great way to stay in touch with current and prospective clients is a newsletter. We send ours by email every quarter. This allows us to get important information out. It can be customized and personalized to what you want to say. You get to create your message.

You can speak directly to your clients. If there is a message that you want to get out, this is an excellent way to do so.

The only noise and fluff that sprouts in a newsletter is up to you. Keep it clean and clear. Don't stick in advertisements or any of that garbage. Otherwise, it will be deleted and ignored. When they see it their opinion has already been made up. They will delete it.

Make the content engaging and relatable to all current and prospective clients. Keep each newsletter new and fresh. Give them a reason to read it. Even better, a reason to make them forward it to their friends or family. Here are a few things that made our newsletter take off:

- Our newsletters are clear and specific. Is your newsletter going to be directly about your business? Or will you tie something unique that everyone can relate to? For instance, will you have a recipe in each newsletter? Will there be an eating or workout tip? Will you review your favorite book or movie? What topic will you tie in so that anyone can relate to it?

• In our newsletter we tied in my favorite book I was reading, restaurant I had been to, movie I had seen, video that grabbed my attention, an app, or item I've come across and enjoyed. I would include the best thing I'd discovered.

• How are you going to keep the reader's attention? You need to make sure it's rather quick and easy to read. Nobody wants to read a newspaper. Emails are not sent to be read as books. Keep every sentence worthwhile.

• Our newsletter only has five topics. The first three are always non-insurance related. The last two are always regarding insurance. We make sure we keep each entry only to a few sentences. The goal is to be able to read the entire newsletter in under a minute.

• What valuable content will I present about my business that makes the newsletter important for them? Will I give them one or two tips each month on how to improve this or that? Give links to what you are reviewing or communicating.

• We included a section about insurance at the end. We had only two entries that pertained to insurance, but they were excellent pieces of information in each newsletter. Do you have this coverage? How is this covered? etc.

• Make sure you put your newsletter together so that you come across as the advisor. You want to be viewed as the expert on whatever industry or product you're relaying to your current and/or prospective clients.

• The two business items pertaining to insurance are very informative. If they were insured with us or another company it would create questions and dialogue. Then, we ask for feedback and questions. We welcome them to contact us.

When I first put our newsletter together, I wanted to send it monthly. But I realized the time it would take to put out great, new, fresh content would be too tough. So, we decided to do it quarterly.

Clients will comment and ask when the next one will come out. It has turned into something that people look forward to getting. Who would ever have thought that a newsletter from your insurance agency would be something you couldn't wait to get? I sure didn't.

The key was we didn't set out for it to be a newsletter. We set out to make it a way to communicate with clients and prospective clients on various topics and ideas that would be intriguing. It was going to be about insurance, but much more than that. Hence why we named it "Insurance & More."

How are you creating conversation and ongoing dialogue with your current and prospective clients? This can be done over email or mail. Email is much cheaper and quicker especially as you build your email database.

Present yourself and your team as the experts. Create content that they find useful and enjoyable to read. Make your opinions, ideas, and tips must-read content.

In our years in business, something we've found to be very beneficial are client reviews. Competing insurance agencies neglect it. When was the last time your insurance agency contacted you to review your policies?

If you operate a business with continual ongoing paying customers, this is an integral part of solidifying that ongoing relationship. Always call your clients before they call you.

In today's world of always looking for new clients we forget about our loyal, continual clients. It's done in all industries. Companies would rather chase new clients than do the best they can for their existing clients. Why is it that a new customer can get a better price than a current customer? Fill in the type company in whichever industry you want. They're all guilty of it.

They all offer better prices to entice new customers while current customers pay more than those offers, and they can't get those offers because they are not "new" clients.

I have never understood this. In our business, the cost to acquire new clients far outweighs the cost in keeping your existing clients. If you lose a ten or twenty-year client, what are the odds that the new clients signing up reach that phase of loyalty with your company? Do what you can to satisfy your current clients. Don't give them a reason to shop your product or service.

When was the last time you checked in with your clients? Offer to review the business that they have with you.

Each year we proactively reach out to our clients to offer a review. We also send an annual informative letter detailing changes in the industry as well as our agency. This offers them the opportunity to consider reviewing the policies they have with us. We will contact them in the early part of the year and then also toward the end of the year. We used to touch base only once every two years, but we found that this approach worked much better. Two contacts a year gives them two opportunities where we reach out to offer them a review.

What I'm doing isn't for everyone or every business, however, if you're considering it, here are a few things that we did differently to keep a constant stream of client reviews.

- Make sure each week your team is contacting the number of people needed to reach all your clients in a year, either by email, calling, or mailing.

- Don't contact just to check the box that you gave them a call. Try to help them do a review. We want to show them the value of reviewing their insurance each year.

- Offer them multiple ways to complete a review. Email, phone call, in person, or video call.

- Have a checklist on everything that you want to cover. Review it with them and have them sign it.

- Be sure to ask if there is anything that your company can do better: What can we improve upon? What would you like to see done differently? You can't improve and get better unless you ask your clients. Otherwise, everything is just a guess.

- Try to keep the review to less than an hour.

Maintain constant client contact and drive home the value that you provide, then you won't have to worry about your clients leaving you. Loyalty is a two-way street.

Referrals and Centers of Influence

What's better than someone referring over a prospective client to you? They come in unexpectedly and usually have a very high closing ratio.

What type of referral program do you have in place for your centers of influence and current customers? How are you capitalizing on people spreading the word about your business?

If someone is willing to speak highly of you and your business, do your best to reward them. Make them feel special.

We like sending gift cards, but sometimes we will send over tickets to a sporting or special event. A custom engraved gift with their name on it goes a long way as well. We've sent books. If you can find ways to allow them to enjoy time with others, such as family and friends, that's even better. Make it a moment not just for that individual, but imagine if it has a lasting memory for their kids?

Don't give items that are engraved or embroidered with your business! You can give these things away to them at any time, but don't give them as a thank you. A thank you with your business info on it isn't really a thank you. It's advertising and everybody knows it.

Also stay away from food as in cookies, cakes, pies, etc. It's really dull. Give more thought than something that says, "I was getting my groceries and realized I should grab you something."

Be sure you keep track of each referral thank you that you give out. If an individual or business is sending over a lot of referrals you need to be sure you give them a proper return thank you. That could be giving an entire building or company lunch as a way to say thank you. Beyond that, keeping track will let you know who's referring who.

To get referrals you must notify your clients that you'd like to get referrals. We send emails to all our current clients twice a year. In addition, we have a letter and postcard that gets mailed.

When a new client signs up, we let them know and also include information about our referral program in their welcome folder.

Whether you're dealing with a client or business as a center of influence you need to ask for referrals. Mention what sort of things you do for thank yous. The closing ratio on referred business is the highest outside of friends and family. The more referrals you receive, the more business you'll get. The conversion ratios prove this. Make it a large point within your business.

Remember to make others speak highly and brag about you and your business. Be a standout!

WOW Gift Program

Few things match the rush of anticipation and excitement of opening a gift. Think back to how you felt the last time you opened a gift not knowing what was inside. Receiving an unexpected gift from someone is one of life's best surprises.

Now ask yourself. When was the last time you gave

an unexpected gift to someone? Why aren't you giving gifts to people who've impacted or helped you in life? Why isn't your business giving gifts to your best clients? It may be time for you to practice the art of gifting.

The most helpful book I've read on gifting is *Giftology* by John Ruhlin. I was looking for ideas to jump start new ways to thank and deepen relationships with our best long-time clients. We would establish a certain level or number of clients and send to them what we called a "WOW gift."

I wanted non-company focused ideas with no advertising on them. The goal was to make it all about my clients and their families. It would have to be something offering a long term impression.

What we decided upon was a personalized city and state specific cutting board. We had sent a cutting board in the past, but this was entirely different.

These would be ordered on an individual basis since you can see it's completely customized. You can imagine the gracious feedback we received.

Stand out and show your clients you care. Go the extra mile.

6

Don't Be Afraid To Stick With What Works

My first boss, Norb Wianecki, would say, "Stick with what works. Don't try to reinvent the wheel. Some tweaks are fine, but many times you get too far away from what was working."

Looking back on successful marketing ideas that we've implemented, it seemed we'd used them for a while, then stopped. Ultimately, and often, we'd circled back to exactly what originally worked and what we'd started with.

Finding good ideas for letters and emails where it generates a response is hard enough. If you find something that's working, build off of it and don't try to start over. It sets you back too much and takes away from continuing to market and send what's working. You'll increase all the extra time to brainstorming and trial, to see if it will work. What does the subject line of the email need to be? What call to action do I want at the end of that letter? All of that, rather than simply continuing to send and follow up on what was working.

Adapting and improving is always important, and I think a willingness to change is necessary. Things change in sales and marketing, when something isn't working, you'll know, but I'll talk more about that later.

When starting out, how do you know what works

and what doesn't? All of that comes from the people that went before you. I learned a lot from Norb and a lot from many others. I learned a lot from my teammates as we worked side by side, building off the foundation given by my mentors. On top of that, I've read a lot of books.

It all comes down to a willingness to learn. The programs we've built are a great success, my clients and peers have told me so. I could let that go to my head, take all the credit, and just be a jerk about it, but I know what really happened. My success was built on the hard work of others that went before me. I may have implemented some good ideas, but without my mentors I would have been years behind where I am now, and who knows, I may have failed entirely. The lessons often saved the day.

While writing this book, I visited two mentors in my life. It had been a long time since I had seen them. To sit and just talk about anything and everything felt so fulfilling. We shared stories and laughs. It was like rekindling old times. Who said you can't go back?

Time passes and everyone ages. We can forget how many years have passed since we've seen certain people. They're busy, you're busy. Who isn't busy?

That evening as I sat down to read, I reflected on the day and smiled. It took a long time to force myself to just set the time aside and make a point to go visit them. I put it on my to do list and got it done. It was gratification at its peak.

What I never understood until years later is how much you reflect and use all those words of wisdom from your mentors. The outlook on life both personally and professionally. What they said all those years ago, now comes into focus. It's taken over 15 years, but now it makes sense. At the time, a lot didn't resonate.

We forget that when mentors tell you things it's coming from their years of experience. Some things they've probably already dealt with. They've traveled the road that you're trying to go down.

As I think back, I wish I would have thought more about what they said. They've experienced life where you are, where you've been, where you're going, or where you want to go. They know what's worth the time and what isn't, and they've just flat out told me the way it is. The outlook on business life and how that blends and reflects into your personal life. They steer and point you in the right direction. Don't forget those directions.

When we're young, we think we're invincible and that we always know best. You hear that often, but I know it's true because that's what I thought. In one ear and out the other. It could have come from mentors or your parents, but damn, I really wish I would have listened or remembered more of what was said to me. They've shared invaluable life lessons.

Spend time with your mentors. Maybe it's even your past teachers. Say thank you and how much you appreciate them. Tell them how much they've helped you. Go see them in person or handwrite a letter to them. Don't wait. I waited too long. I wish I would have done it sooner.

If you have the ability or chance to be a mentor, do it. My mentors made such an impact on me that I hope someday I can have a similar impact on someone else. Their impact will last far beyond me. My children will feel their impact. Their children will feel their impact.

Embrace the chance. You're giving life changing advice and wisdom whether you realize it or not. Many years from now, they'll still remember and use a lot of what you tell them. I do every day of my life.

We should all strive to mentor others and make that same impact. Ask yourself, are you making an impact on someone else's life?

Part 2
Start

7

High School

I will be the first to admit I didn't like school. I didn't put much effort into my schoolwork. It just wasn't something that I could see helping me in the future. Do you know the feeling? The feeling that it just isn't going to matter or help? That is how I felt.

I got along great with my teachers. Many I knew very well outside of school. I didn't cause trouble or skip school, but I just liked talking with the teachers and my fellow students, usually about last night's sporting events. That was the highlight of my day. I couldn't have cared less what Mr. Waters was going to teach me about biology. That was a subject I hated and knew I would never use in my life… ever. And I have yet too. I only took the class because Mr. Waters was my baseball coach and we got along.

What did I do all day in class? A lot of time was spent searching sports information and trying to improve my fantasy sports teams, but I would also read. That is one thing I did every day. Probably more than most of my classmates. I read finance magazines and periodicals, *USA Today*, *Barron's*, and *The Wall Street Journal*.

My mind was becoming a sponge for financial information. I loved it and couldn't get enough. Yes, a weirdo, I know. Many of my friends thought the same. What I was learning was real life events and how the stock market worked, what drove the economy and the world. Yes, learning biology was important to some, but not me. I wanted to learn more about business and what moved the financial system. I read to learn. I wanted to absorb all of it.

Beginning Of My Path

When you enter my office, this quote from Ralph Waldo Emerson greets you: "Do not go where the path may lead, go instead where there is no path and leave a trail."

As a sophomore in high school, I was helping my dad finish off our basement. We got to talking about careers and I started telling him how in awe I was of business. We talked about insurance, and I explained what I had been reading. He could tell I was taking a liking to numbers and working with people. I loved to talk with people of all ages. It was my dad who first brought up being an insurance adjuster. That sounded interesting. He mentioned that I should go see our local family friend, Norb Wianecki, who owned his own business downtown. He owned an insurance agency that represented American Family Insurance. It sounded good to me.

It just so happened, a few weeks later, the career development class I was in required us to conduct a job shadow. Our teacher would make the contact for us at a local employer for a job that interested us. As many of my friends and classmates selected policemen, teachers, radio stations, or their parents, I decided to shadow Norb.

When I went to see him, I think he was surprised and

somewhat shocked. What the heck does a high school kid want to know about insurance? I had a lot of questions. How does it all work? What does an adjuster do? What does he do?

When I got insight from someone that was actually working in the insurance industry, I knew I would like it. You get to help people when they're in need and make a great living. Plus, you run your own business and the opportunities are endless. You get what you put into it. Like any business.

The next school year I moved into a school-to-work program with Norb and his office assistant, Lisa Hanson. I would work at his office two hours a day.

Then, my senior year, I moved it up to four hours a day. Instead of going to school, I was going to work with Norb for half the school day. And oh, did my classmates hate me.

I was learning so much and my knowledge of insurance was growing. I loved it! The more I learned, the more I knew what I wanted to do. I knew I could do this and I'm going to do a damn good job at it.

After that school year ended, working for Norb turned into a full time job. I was now working there year-round. Under the school-to-work program I wasn't being paid. My friends that did the same thing at their jobs were. I wasn't, but that didn't bother me. I was learning and sometimes a price can't be put on knowledge you are bound to use.

Then I remember the day Norb told me he was going to start paying me. I would get minimum wage $6.15 an hour. Then, once licensed, I would get paid commissions. I was eager, "When can I get that," I asked.

July 17, 2003, I went and passed my insurance licensing exam. The proctor where I took the test told me I was the youngest person at the time to ever get their insurance license in WI. I was 18 and three months old. I was ready to rock n' roll.

After graduation, I went to work with Norb full time and took a couple insurance classes at the local technical college. One was to obtain my INS designation (Certificate in General Insurance) and the other was the AIS (Associate in Insurance Services) designation.

In addition, I took a personal finance class. That is still the single most beneficial and important class I have ever taken. I still have the course book on my bookshelf to this day. My Dad took the class with me. We learned so much from that class. Looking back, it was one of the coolest things that my Dad and I did together. We had a great time driving up to school together listening to the baseball games and then stopping somewhere to eat. They're memories that neither of us will forget.

From there, things accelerated. I was selling and, not only that, I was knocking the cover off the ball. And I was starting to get interested in starting my own insurance agency.

I talked with management at American Family Insurance about starting my own business.

Norb's district manager, Paul Swalve told me what I needed to do, but cautioned me a bit as I was only 19 at the time.

I went through the next available agent-in-training program. Now I had the company training needed to embark on my dream to run my own insurance agency and I knew I wanted to represent American Family Insurance.

They were good to me and helped me get started. I felt a bit of gratitude and loyalty to them. Taking a chance on me, spending the money and company resources to help train me. I wanted to repay American Family, Paul Swalve, and Norb Wianecki by being one of the best to ever do it.

On April 1, 2008, four years later, I moved up to Neenah, Wisconsin to start my agency. It was a very small agency I was taking over, but that didn't matter to me. I had the opportunity I'd dreamed of. That was the part of Wisconsin I've always wanted to live and have my business. The door was cracked and now it was my time to blow it wide open and take off. And take off we did!

We've grown to be one of the largest insurance agencies by policies in the country. My team and I have worked hard, put in many endless hours of hard work, but we've had a lot of fun doing it.

I started with one assistant and have since expanded from just the two of us in a 609 square foot office with no windows, to now having multiple offices with a lot of windows. We now have marketing, sales, and service departments.

The accolades that the team has accomplished are astounding. We've set a 90-year company record at American Family for the most life insurance policies sold in a single year. We've been Agency of the Year, Championship Ring Holder, multiple year recipients of the Centurion Award, Premier Leader Award, and All-American Award. Along with many others.

Thanks to American Family Insurance. They have

rewarded me for doing my job and taking care of my clients.

These are all things I'm extremely proud of, but, more importantly, I love my job more than ever and can't wait to wake up every day to go to the office. I can't wait to get in with my team to embark on our next journey together. They're all like family to me.

8

Sleeping On Your Office Floor

Don't let anyone ever tell you that starting a business is easy. The hours you have to put in get so long sometimes that the only thing that makes sense is sleeping on your office floor.

One of the toughest night's sleep of my life was the night before I opened my business. I traded a bed that night for my office floor. For my pillow, I used a rolled-up sheet that I used to cover things while transporting them to my office. In all, I probably got about three hours of sleep.

Failure was not going to be an option. I wanted to be one of the best to do it. If I was going to fail it wasn't going to be because I didn't work hard enough. I may not have been the smoothest salesman or known everything about insurance, but nobody was going to outwork me.

That first morning I was at Walmart at 5 AM picking up Pepto-Bismol, a toothbrush, toothpaste, and mouthwash. Yes, quite a combination and way to start your first day in business.

A few years later, when we moved out of that small 609 square foot office space, I came across that bottle of Pepto-Bismol, toothbrush, toothpaste and mouthwash. I had put it in a mirrored vanity that I forgot even opened. I'd only used them that first morning, then it all sat in there.

At that moment, it really made me think of the leap I had taken. I'd come a long way from the anxiety, fear of the unknown, and fear of failure on that first morning.

What type of opportunity or challenges have been laid before you? Have you created excuses to not pursue your dreams? Are you afraid of failure?

Start charting your path today. Roll up your sleeves, get started, and succeed. Improve your life and the life of your family. Reach, then reach higher. Become one of the best!

If you have that dream or pie in the sky idea, take the time to pursue it. Before work, after work, or during lunch, start researching and spending time at it. If you need to quit or change jobs to allow you to pursue it, then do it. If you fall and fall again it doesn't matter how hard you fall it's that you keep getting up. Pull yourself up, dust yourself off, then forge ahead.

You learn and improve through failure and rejection. Nobody makes every shot. You will forever regret the shots that you don't take and ask yourself what if. Don't be that person. Take that shot.

9

Gameplan To Starting Your Business

Before you spend any money, use your time to work up a business plan. Lay out the main objective of your business. Is it to sell a product? Are you selling a service such as lawn care?

Will you be buying into a franchise? No matter what it is, a proper thought-out business plan is the very first thing that you need to do. Walk before you run.

What should your business plan entail? It will depend somewhat on what it is your business will do. I'm going to share with you some of my business plan when I looked at starting my insurance agency, but I don't want to lay out everything that I did, because your business will be and should be different, even if you sell insurance.

Building a business is like building a house. Start with a blueprint. Every house then needs a foundation. Then add your footings and walls that give support to the entire house. View your business the same way.

Your plan when finding a location is just like when you want to build a house and often determines what your business can look like. You'll draw up a floor plan for a home and it's the same for your business. The blueprint will show how the business will look years down the road. Your foundation is your team. Without a great foundation, the house will crumble, and it's the same with your team. The structure is how it all operates.

The most important part of the home-building process is the planning stage. It's the same in business. The plan and blueprint for your business is essential to success. I had a one-year plan, five-year plan, and dream plan. The dream plan is like building your dream home, but make sure your dream plan is realistic and attainable. After all, that is the ultimate goal you'll be chasing.

Everyone's eventual goal is to hit their dream plan. Many years down the road you will experience the "we finally did it" feeling. It's feeling on top of the mountain and thinking to yourself, "ok what do we do next?"

To get there, you need to talk to an experienced builder. Truth is, before you start a business, take the time to speak to people who have done it. Lean on their experience. Ask questions to help create your plan of action. After speaking with my mentors, I started to get a plan together.

At each stage, I set markers I had to reach to show it was working. That we were doing something right. Some go without saying, but I'll also share a few things I've learned along the way.

Year One

Starting out, I knew I just had to make sure I sold enough to grow and make it. I had to make all the people that went to bat for me and helped me along the way proud. Failure was not an option.

I needed to make sure I had a good location for people to find my office and a good person on staff to help me. The goal was to try and sell enough to hire a second team member. I knew that to eventually get where I wanted to go, and fast, I needed to find good people to help me.

I had to keep an eye out for someone that I could convince to come work for a young guy who just started an insurance business. In summary, I just wanted to make it. I just needed to sell enough to be able to eat and pay rent.

Head down and push forward. The first year just feels like an uphill climb. It can be hard to see very well in the middle of it all, but hard work and persistence pay off.

Something that I'm glad I did very early on was try new ideas. When you talk to your mentors, others in your industry, or leaders in your field, take note. Take note, but don't anchor to everything you're told by others. Tweak, change, and adapt your plan to what you want. That may mean being different from all the others. It may seem like you're on an island trying something new, and that's ok.

Instead, take what they tell you and be better. If everyone's doing the same thing, try to be different. If you're running with the crowd, you are like everyone else. The goal is not being average or fitting in, but being different. Stand out from the crowd.

Blaze your own trail. Spend time outworking everyone else. If they are all going right, go left. Eventually everyone will be going right and there will be no advantage in doing the same.

You will not be able to stand out and be great. You will just blend in. So, go the opposite direction.

As you learn from your mentors and read

biographies of the most successful people, you'll soon realize that they were way out on an island doing something different to become pioneers and trailblazers. Everyone soon wanted to follow their trail. At the time, they were doing what everyone considered different, weird, or would never work.

In my years in business, I'd often try something that was against the grain and different. When people responded with skepticism and would question why I was doing it, I knew I was onto something.

My ideas and programs were crafted by me and my team. When we rolled out something new and different and found others following our lead, I knew what we'd come up with, that was viewed as different and not worth our time, sure was worth it. Once others started following our lead, I knew it was time to start looking at the next different idea.

Let others question you. Blaze that trail. Make others follow you. Break barriers. Don't be afraid and if you fall, get up and try again. The one way to not break barriers is to not try. Try that crazy idea, or thing that's not being done. Be different.

Year Five

In five years I wanted to have a sales team and a service team. I knew if we were still around in five years, we would have done something right.

At the five-year mark I did have a service team of two and a sales team of one. It started to show me how to manage a larger team and everything I learned helped prepare me for when I grew that team to twelve people.

I wanted to be able to have any loans or business lines of credit paid off. My business would be off the ground and debt free. So, if I wanted to buy another agency, my finances were in line. I would not be looked at as a startup or saddled with a large debt load. I wanted to have a cash flow where, if we went into debt, we were well capitalized and had a renewal income base to handle any purchases or acquisitions.

At this point, people can go in many different directions. What happens most often is expansion. Bigger is better, right? Honestly, bigger isn't good or bad. It's an option. If that's what you want your business to be, go for it! The problem I've seen in many businesses is that things get too complicated. This can happen in big and small businesses. What I've found great value in is a simple idea: reduce decisions.

It's well documented that many successful people wear the same exact clothes every day. Albert Einstein wore several variations of the same suit. Mark Zuckerberg does the same with his t-shirt and jeans. Steve Jobs famously did as well with his black turtleneck.

"You'll see I wear only gray or blue suits," President Barack Obama shared with Michael Lewis in Vanity Fair, "I'm trying to pare down decisions. I don't want to make decisions about what I'm eating or wearing. Because I have too many other decisions to make. You need to focus your decision-making energy. You need to routinize yourself. You can't be going through the day distracted by trivia."

If this works for Albert Einstein, Mark Zuckerberg, Steve Jobs and Barack Obama, shouldn't it work for you?

Be a creature of habit. Minimize decision making. Try to eliminate as many decisions as possible. Save that brain power for things that really matter. Stop the time spent on unproductive and unprofitable activities. Look at where your time goes and how it is spent. Cut out the fat.

Spend the time doing what you love. Fulfill your purpose. Drive the goals you want.

Start to find routines and habits that reduce your decision making. Allow yourself to be totally set on making important decisions. Don't find yourself standing, looking at your closet of clothes, trying to determine what to wear.

The Dream

Many would add a ten-year plan, but I didn't. I labeled it a dream plan. That was my ultimate goal to chase. This plan will change, because the dream scenario and our ultimate goals that far out, do change along the way.

My dream plan was to own and operate multiple insurance agencies. I wanted to be among the largest agencies in the country. Then, I wanted to eventually set the record for most life insurance sold in a single year.

I remember looking at these goals as really having "dream on," "yeah right," and "that'll never happen" reactions. If I had told these to others, they probably would have agreed. It wouldn't have been just me. Any agency owner would have said those things and laughed.

In 2016, after eight years in business we achieved

all of this in the same year. This was in addition, and all a distance second, to the birth of our first child.

I was in the process of opening a second location when she was born. A lot of decisions were made while at home with my wife and daughter during those first few weeks after her birth. All in between feeding time and trying to find time to sleep. That was wild!

Then, at the end of that year, we broke the company record to become the new leader in life insurance sales in a single year for American Family. We were also among the largest agencies. Whenever I think about 2016, I smile. That was a year I'll never forget.

What would you do if you achieved your dream? Would you lean back and put your feet on the desk, saying mission accomplished? Do you have the feeling that you've crossed the finish line?

Maybe for the day or hour you could do that. Take some time and live in the moment.

Take a vacation or do something for you, your family, and team that made it happen.

Then what? Don't get too comfortable or you could end up going backwards and the dream you've made could dissolve. Look at all the companies who were at the top of their industry over the years, only to fail.

The company that I always think of is Blockbuster Video. They were very popular to me growing up. Blockbuster was the place that everyone went to rent movies all over the world. It seemed like they were on every block.

But they never adapted to the consumers changing their renting habits. Video streaming and on demand rental forced them into bankruptcy and to close all its stores.

Blockbuster was in their dream plan and had succeeded but didn't stay on top of their game. They didn't adapt to what their customers wanted.

Don't get to the top and then fall back down. You need to continue to innovate and adapt to the ever-changing marketplace. It doesn't wait. It will move right on without you.

Grow, evolve and be at the cutting edge of your industry. When you stop growing and stop listening to your customers, you will fail.

I'm a huge advocate for purchasing and reading as much industry news as possible.

Regardless of what you're selling or what type of business you're running, you need to keep up with the latest and greatest ideas and innovation.

My dad owns a plumbing business. Imagine the type of change that he sees and encounters. It really isn't all that different from my insurance business. We both see changes to current products and new trends coming. Some may just be temporary and may not stick, but we need to be educated on these trends and changes so we can accurately explain them to our clients.

It's true that knowledge is power. The more you know the better you're armed and dangerous in any business. The customer you're speaking with sees that you're not just a salesman, but an adviser and educator.

If you explain the positive and negative of this product compared with the other and relate it to their situation, that's what people ultimately want to hear. They realize you're a student of your industry and have their best interests in mind.

Consumers want you to be honest with them. They

want an honest person selling them a good product at a fair price. Sounds simple, doesn't it? Well, some of the best have got to the top shortly before they fell. The lesson is to stay hungry.

10

No College Degree

When I tell people I didn't go to college, many are shocked. "What do you mean you didn't go to college?" Well, sorry to disappoint you. Then the common follow up question is, "Then, how did you get so much knowledge about business, insurance, and investing at such a young age?"

Sometimes people ask if I took over a family business. Their first thought is that I must have been handed something. Everyone jumps to a conclusion that you must have had an "in," that you found an easy road. Take a logical question, then follow it up with an assumption, implying that someone had an easy path. If you see someone who's very rich, they must have inherited or won the money. To me both assumptions are a slap in the face.

Something I've learned is if you are going to make assumptions, keep them to yourself. It doesn't pay to alienate or make someone angry with blurting out an assumption.

To the question of where I obtained my knowledge if not in going to school. My answer isn't anything special, I hate to say. I gathered it from books, trial and error, and experience. I read books upon books, then took the information I learned in those books and tried it out.

I would discover ideas and new ways of doing

things, then I could experiment with what worked best and what didn't. It was like my own laboratory. The books I read were better than my textbooks from school. That's how I viewed them. These are my textbooks that are going to show me how to be the best at this or learn to do that correctly.

So, I read. I probably read too much sometimes. It almost became an addiction. Once I found what was available in books, I knew I could really learn anything. On top of that, I could learn whatever I wanted from the best in the world. Whoever was or is the best at something probably wrote a book about it, or someone wrote it about them.

The greatest people in every industry are studied and well documented. You just have to seek them out. Get as many books as possible. Have a mini library in your home. Your decor is books!

Trying Is Your Best Teacher

You often hear the phrases "trial and error," "learning on the job," or "you learn by making mistakes." These are ways that you learn and improve in any job. You can read out of a book or watch YouTube videos all day and night. But until you actually do it, you will not know what obstacles come up.

Schooling and learning are a great foundation, but will only take you so far. You will not truly learn if you're good at something or what your future holds until you roll up your sleeves and get to work. When you make a mistake and fail, how do you respond? What are you going to do differently the next time to avoid that mistake?

Starting off in sales I made a lot of mistakes. I had given quotes to households where I traveled to their home, wrote their insurance, only to find my rates were inaccurate and came back much higher.

One time they were ineligible, and I couldn't write their insurance at all. That call to the customer to tell them was tough. When they said they had already canceled their previous company it was even harder. It got resolved, but was a fantastic learning experience for an 18-year-old just starting out in sales.

Sales is something very hard to teach. "How tos" don't help much. It's extremely unpredictable. It's based entirely on a conversation with someone. The objections, subject material, and rapport, among other things, can go so many ways that you can't possibly explain, teach, or cover everything prior to an appointment or sales call.

Why do you think so many times you hear people say "I wasn't cut out for sales"? I get it all the time when I interview for positions within my agency. Many people are scared away by the word. It intimidates them. If you have never done it, or did, but had zero success, I don't blame you. Sales are not easy. If that wasn't the case, everyone would do it, because, in most industries, sales have limitless income.

The Power Of Books

What you can learn and uncover for $10 to $20. What's the best return of any purchase of your life? Where else can you get that kind of life-changing return on investment?

Naval Ravikant, an angel investor and CEO of

Angellist, said on a Tim Ferriss podcast interview, "I would say the real education begins in the library. It begins with books. If you can learn to like to read, you never need to go to school."

Someone with that type of success who went to Dartmouth, to state something like that really reinforces the power, knowledge, and information that can be found in books. I am not saying skip college and just read books, but the opportunity is knocking on everyone's front door. Anyone can improve any area of their life whether it be personal or professional.

As I've stated previously, my extent of higher education after high school was very little.

I attended a technical college to take a few classes as I had scholarship money to use. In all, I ended up taking that one semester of classes and that was my extent of higher education.

My focus was back at my office where I was trying to chart a path to owning my own insurance agency. I was spending time at the office from 7:30 am to 6:00 pm. At home on the weekends, I was working on trying to find ideas and concepts to make me successful.

I read books and went online when it would connect. These were still the dial up days, which means I couldn't be on too long, because when you were on the internet the home phone didn't work. This was obviously before the rise of cell phones as well.

Each Saturday I was making a trip over to the local Book World. I was buying as many sales and finance books as I could find. Eventually, I learned about Amazon when it was still mainly a book seller and couldn't believe how easy it was. I was ordering books four or five at a time.

Every morning and night I was reading. I was trying to find any advantages I could. I also read biographies from famous business leaders. What did they do that made them successful?

This is where my knowledge came from. I didn't sit in a classroom for hours. I didn't spend thousands of dollars on sales seminars only to still ask questions at the end of the day, then buy the presenters books, videos, and tapes. I found that there was no quick and easy route. This was going to take time and a ton of hard work.

Learning insurance, sales, and running a business were not the only subjects that I turned to books to learn. Investing and finance also really interested me.

A large portion of my collection of books are on money and investing. Just because you have your own financial advisor or investor doesn't mean you have to be clueless on how they are investing and managing your money for you. You may just find that the person you have is watching out for their best interests and investing your money in what makes them the most money and not you. I wanted to have a vast knowledge of the financial markets and know how the best investors invested.

The hundreds of books that I have read are displayed on the shelves in my home office.

Others line the shelves at my offices. That personal financial planning course book from the technical college among them.

My books are a reminder of all the time and commitment I put in to educate myself to be successful. A reminder that your learning is never done. I have met people who read a book a day. These people lead large companies and make more than enough money, yet still read daily.

Read and read some more. Never stop educating yourself. Buy books new or used.

Hardcover, paperback, audiobook, or whatever, it doesn't matter. Start your own library on your bookshelf or on your phone. Just become a sponge for information.

If you start a book and it just isn't doing anything for you, you're not learning anything, or it's boring, then toss it aside and start another. Start skimming ahead to see if it starts to click for you. Reading a book should not be a drag or be boring. If it is, time to donate the book. Don't toss it, donate it because it may resonate or speak to someone else. If you look forward to opening a book you're reading, then you know you're on the right path. Don't be afraid to stop a book.

My wife got me hooked on Audible. Audiobooks have been very popular for a long time, but I kept wanting to read books in the actual physical form.

She started listening to books while she did laundry and got ready in the mornings. All of sudden she was finishing fiction novels in under a week. These were books that were 8, 10, or 12 hours long. How the heck is she doing that?

If you went ahead and added up all the time you could be listening to a book, you'd be amazed. Drive time adds up each day.

I had listened to sports talk radio or music. Then, I took that time to listen to books. Look at your day. I did and found a ton of time that could be focused on a book.

Podcasts are another item that I've now worked into

this time. I used to think of it as dead time, but now I look forward to it. Now I'm flying through a book per week.

Before this, I was growing frustrated. I was having a hard time finding the time to sit down and read a book. With having little kids, that time was nonexistent. My wife had gone many months without reading a book.

Excuses no more! And there shouldn't be any excuses for anyone else. If you bike to work, drive to work, or ride the subway, you have a starting point right there. Once you do that, you'll be amazed at the amount of time you find to power through books.

If you need help with something, what do you do? If you want to improve and become the best you can at something, what would you do? You would try to talk and learn from the best. Right?

Well, what if that best person in the world had a book? Maybe the five or ten best in the world at sales all have a book out sharing their insights. Wouldn't you read it, take notes, and implement what they say? Damn right, you would. So, what are you waiting for? Want to get better at something? Then put the work in. Become a student of that subject. Nobody is just born the best. They work at it and learn how to become the best.

When I was starting my business, the "I don't know how" or "I don't know enough" excuses weren't going to fly. The success of my business was solely up to me.

I didn't know how to hire employees or what having employees all entailed. I didn't know how to market a business or create a marketing plan. I had to teach myself and figure out what worked and didn't work. If

I wanted to find out how other entrepreneurs became successful, I knew there was only one road.

The information I learned through reading was put to use through trial and error. It's the only way I learned. Some things didn't work for me, other things got me to where I am today and changed my life.

Today, I have 398 books that fill my shelves. Whenever I come across a book that looks like something I want to read, I buy it. If someone recommends a book to me, I buy it. Some books are worth completing. Others are not. If you aren't learning or a book isn't holding your interest, move on to the next.

I can't begin to count the number of books that I've given to people over the years. How many of them get read? I have no idea. Books need to be viewed like you've just been handed the answers to an upcoming test by your teacher. People need to think of books as the answers to their problems, the path to improvement. I'm writing this book due to the books I read about writing. Nobody taught me how to write. I just knew it was something that I wanted to do. I researched and found the best books on the subject.

If you have a passion for something then find a way. If you want to improve, don't make excuses. Just find a way and do it. You have millions of books, or should I say teachers, waiting to help you out.

11

Dream Big, Nobody Else Will For You

Growing up all I heard was "Chase your dreams. Dream big." What does that really mean? How big should someone dream? Then they would tell you to have a vision to get there. Whatever. Easier said than done.

When you have a dream, you really do need vision to get there. Why? Because nobody else is going to draw you a map on how to reach it. There is no compass that will point you to the destination of your dream.

Most will not be able to help you with this because they've never reached their dream.

I learned this early on. I needed to dream big because nobody else would for me. People can give you ideas and suggestions for things you should do or invent or create, but nobody knows what you really want to do other than you.

When I knew what my vision was to reach my dream, I had to block out all the noise and the misconception that others would do it for me. Block out the idea that the government or anyone else will take care of you. The world is not going to hand you anything.

If you want to earn money, have a good job, and a nice house, then you better be ready and prepared to work. You need to start planning and have that vision early.

If you wait, you'll stall and fall behind. Have that confidence in yourself and what you're doing. Getting the proper mindset is very important. Get your head right!

It's not just in starting something, but also in trying to improve yourself a little bit each day. We all make mistakes and have dumb moments. Take these moments and use them as a learning experience to improve yourself as a human being. If you don't learn from your mistakes and adapt to change things for the better, you're not growing.

It's challenging, but remember to view failures, losses, and rejection as ways to improve and get better. Fix, change, improve, and train yourself to be the best.

Early To Wake, Early To Win

Sleep is one of the most loved things in many people's lives. Very few things make people as happy as sleeping. How would you react if tonight when you went to bed and set your alarm that it changed and went off at 5:00 am? How hard would you slam your phone or toss it across the room? Heck, for most people their day would be ruined. How dare something interrupt my sleep!

My morning starts every day at 5:00 am. I know, many think I'm crazy, but if I get between six and seven hours of sleep, I'm ready to roll. If I get more than seven hours of sleep, I feel tired and sluggish that day. It seems odd, but it happens every time.

I used to sleep in until the absolute last minute before I had to go to school or work. I was gaining weight during this time as well. My life was sitting in an office after years of playing sports every day.

I knew that I had to improve my lifestyle and that started with working out.

The hardest part in starting to workout is identifying a time to do it. Then actually doing it! Some may fit it in over their lunch hour. I chose the early morning. I like my nights free to do as I please.

I started setting my alarm earlier and earlier. It started with 7:00. After a month I increased it by a half hour and again with the next and the next until I settled on 5:00. This allowed me the proper time to get everything done that I wanted to and still be in my office around 7:00 each day.

Once this started to become a habit, I started to lose weight and increased my productivity and sales at work. I felt the best I had ever felt. I started this at 230 pounds. Now years later I'm at 195 pounds. I didn't lose it all at once but over the course of a year.

Everything was better and I felt great. Food tasted better. Your mentality and outlook on everything changes, and, believe it or not, you'll have more energy and focus when you hold yourself to a schedule, workout, and eat well.

Early to rise, early to grind. Wake up ready to roll and kick ass. That has been my outlook when that alarm goes off and I think to myself, "Ten more minutes" or "I think I'll take today off." Go work out and get going while others sleep. Work and work harder while your competitor's sleep. There is no substitute for hard work.

That starts with your mentality. Get your day set and then execute. When you wonder why you are not achieving your goals, think about what you have done to change and achieve them? Look in the mirror. The only person to answer to is yourself and the only person to hold you accountable is yourself. The only excuse is your laziness! Get off your ass and move!

My workouts change and vary. I use my Peloton for spin, yoga, strength training, and meditation. I play basketball and run for three to four miles outside. Those are all important and enjoyable but my favorite and most beneficial workout I do is practicing yoga.

My early mornings start with working out. That may not be the best time for you, but whatever you do, begin to introduce an early start to your day. I think you'll be shocked at how beneficial it can be.

Routine

"Routine, in an intelligent man, is a sign of ambition. A modern stoic knows that the surest way to discipline passion is to discipline time: decide what you want or ought to do during the day, then always do it at the same moment every day, and passion will give you no trouble."

W.H. Auden

My normal day is filled with a rather simple routine. As I mentioned, I get up at 5:00 and workout, first thing in the morning. By 7:00 I'm usually having a coffee and reading. I'll first read the news and catch up on important events across the business and investing world. Then I'll read a book for about fifteen minutes.

This seems to help get my brain in gear. From here I dive into my businesses, verify my to-do list, and clear out and answer my emails. I check in with my team, and make sure all is set for the day.

I will then embark on my deep-thinking activities all morning long. This is when I feel the sharpest and get my best thinking and brainstorming done. Usually around mid-morning I will have a midday snack and destress from things a bit.

After that I'll dig into reviewing current systems to make sure things are on point. This is when I will do some meetings with my team and dig into their ideas. We'll also brainstorm together.

At lunch, I usually leave for an hour. I get away to be alone. It's a search for peace and quiet. I have a few lunch spots that I like to go to after 1:00. Most places are cleared out and the lunch rush is over. I realized, instead of scrolling through twitter or wasting time on sports related things, I could spend my lunch time reading.

Using this extra time to read, I now find myself being able to finish books much faster.

Because of this I can finish a book in a couple days instead of a couple of weeks. I've found that I can absorb what I'm reading during this time more than any other time of the day.

After lunch I will reach out and contact the people that I need to speak or meet with. At about 3:30, as I have my afternoon green tea, I will embark on goals and dig into my writings and self-improvement practices. I'll set up what needs to be done tomorrow and plan.

Then at around 5:00 my day is complete. I turn it off and head home to my wife and kids.

Usually, I'm home around 5:30. The evenings are

my family time. I will periodically, a couple times an evening, just glance at my emails to be sure nothing urgent has come up.

Being able to unplug is one of the most underrated things when you're in business.

Realistically you could operate and go 24/7. There is always something to be done or worked on. Things always need improvement and new programs to be started. You could always fix and update existing programs. You can be a perfectionist, where nothing is ever good enough.

Having a wife and kids really tests those boundaries and I've needed to find a way to turn off the business side of my brain at a certain time each night. It's healthy and needed for my sanity.

If you want to have a great family life, you need to adopt a work and home life balance.

By not doing this, your personal life will suffer. Besides, you will just be happier and so will your family. So Just Do It!

After everyone goes to bed, I will usually spend time writing. I view this as my creative time. It's the time I worked on writing this book. This is also the time I write for my blog, *Spilled Coffee*, on Substack.

How many routines do you have? Think about your day. How many things are done without giving any thought? Some days I wake up and realize I'm working out, then find myself with a coffee in my hand at my desk. I will wake up and those things just occur. They have become daily routines. That is the start of my day every day of the week. I find that working out clears my head and relaxes my mind. Stress seems to just drip away.

I've found that routines fight away stress. Whether the routines are working out, making the same thing for breakfast, or going to the same place for lunch every day. It saves brain power for working on important decisions. It frees up your time to solely focus on what you want to work on. Conquer your current mission.

The quote above from W.H. Auden explains this perfectly. The more routines that I find instilled into my life, the more focus I have for what I'm working on, and the less decisions I must make in a day.

Why wouldn't you eliminate as many decisions as possible? Make your decision-making energy worth it. Establish routines now.

Plan Tomorrow Today

At the end of each day, before I leave my desk or go to bed, I will make a list of what I need to get done tomorrow. I'll have my calendar pulled up to see what I have scheduled and when I'll need to get certain things done. I will block out chunks of time during the day to get everything done. All my teammates can see the whole team's calendars. When I have time blocked out, they know nothing can be scheduled during those times. You need to approach your schedule this way.

When I first started in business, I didn't do this. Then, when I evaluated my use of time, I failed miserably. It felt like my days were going by in a split second and I wasn't getting anything done. The important things I needed to do were not getting completed.

I started planning tomorrow today and made sure I

was not allowing time-wasting activities to eat up my time. Start it now.

If you are new to your job or just starting a business, get in the habit now. You'll be way ahead. Most end up needing to fix and delegate things once they're already in business and feel overworked and are not completing the important tasks.

Force yourself to schedule tomorrow today. Make a to do list and mark out chunks of time in your schedule to complete everything. If something is not worth your time, don't do it. Does it need to be done? Pass it along to someone whose time is better spent doing it. Then you can attack the things that will produce important results.

Change

In both your personal and professional life, you're going to come across change. Change will happen daily for you.

Change happens so fast today that something could change in the morning and by the afternoon you need to have a firm handle on all of it. Then, next month it could turn upside down again. You will experience minor changes and also an entire change with how you conduct business. This could happen overnight or within weeks, months, or years. With the amount of competition across industries now, you must be on top of your game.

Through the years, I've spent time with many other business owners. I learned how they view and handle change. People that don't adjust to change or make their business adapt to it, die a slow death. That means, if it's not evolving and growing, it's falling behind. Once you start to fall behind it's like climbing a mountain to try and get back to the level they were.

So, as change happens, don't push back. You can complain for a few minutes, but then you'd better figure out how you're going to deal with this change. It could be something that hurts your sales performance and competitiveness in the marketplace, or it could be on the customer service side. Always be willing to try new systems and processes. Here are some questions you may need to ponder:

- Do I need to scale back my sales or service team?
- Do I need to look at hiring more help?
- Do I need to dive back into the day-to-day operations?
- Do I need to delegate more?
- Do I have to do some more training directly with my team on sales or marketing ideas to drive more sales?
- Do I or my team need new training with this change?
- Does my brand and direct marketing plans need to change?
- Has our target customer changed?
- Do I have to consider a new service or operating system for the business?

This list could go on and on. It's almost like a brainstorming exercise for yourself. Set a list of things that could go wrong in your business and write down how you would react and what the plan would be if that happened. It's being prepared for the storm before it hits.

I have a large file dedicated to agency workflow, procedures, and guidelines. In it, I detail how all our programs work, who is responsible, how often, and how to do them. Then, in case someone leaves, I have all our processes and duties documented. When the new person comes in, they have their playbook on what they are to do and how to follow our agency procedures. This allows everyone to be consistent and provides the way to do things how I want. Now, if there is a change or improvement needed, I will go in and update the file.

Embrace and move with change. Otherwise, you're going to be left behind. Continue to innovate and evolve. If you don't keep up and try to stay ahead of your competitors, you're going to get passed by.

<h1 style="text-align:center">12</h1>

Stop Making Excuses and Start Building

In a world caught up in complaining about nearly everything, we find ourselves wasting too many minutes, hours, and days on such mindless, time-wasting activities. We push our complaints on others. We air our dirty laundry on social media, which turns into more mindless, time-wasting activity.

How is any of this helping you to take action on your goals? What are you building by wasting your time complaining?

Complaining prevents action. Complaining is a way to cling to excuses to prevent taking action. Stop finding things to complain about. There will always be something to complain about. You can always find a way to be negative about anything.

The act of complaining breeds excuses which creates negativity. It's this vicious growth that ends up holding you back. It definitely doesn't breed productivity. It destroys goals and aspirations.

People will say things like, "I don't have the time to do that. Maybe someday I will." Or you'll get the denier, saying things like, "I can't do that. I don't know how to do that. It's impossible."

Do these words come from you? Are you someone who instantly tells yourself that you can't do something before even trying it? Your instinct shouldn't automatically default to telling yourself no or finding excuses to not do something.

Excuses only get in your way. Nothing is achieved by complaining. Instead of spending your time and brain power on complaining, excuses, and negativity, try asking yourself the following:

- How am I using my time?
- What am I working towards?
- What's my ultimate goal?
- Am I making strides every day and every week to reach my ultimate goal?

"I'm too busy," is one of the biggest excuses I hear. It always makes me wonder, is that an honest answer? Or is it just taking the easy way out? Really what you're saying is that it just isn't important enough to do.

In Tim Ferriss's book *Tribe of Mentors*, Debbie Millman speaks to the topic of being busy, "Busy is a decision," she says plainly. She continues, "If we use busy as an excuse for not doing something, what we are really, really saying is that it's not a priority. Simply put: You don't *find* the time to do something; you *make* the time to do things." Millman states (emphasis added).

Maybe you're waiting for the perfect time. But when is that time? Who lets you know?

There is never a perfect time. So stop waiting.

Start doing. Many will say they want to do something, but won't actually do it. They're afraid of taking action. Take action! Get off your ass and actually do it. Create! Build! Aspire!

All the opportunities are available to you.

Technology, tools, and resources are more accessible today than any other time in history. You just need the drive and desire.

Start going after what you aspire to be or do. If you don't like something, change it! Do you think you can do something better? Do it! Build a business. Build a story. Build a legacy. Just start building.

Get what you want to do at the top of your list. The things that you truly want to do, you'll do. Stop trying to please others and make your "busy time" your time.

If someone asks you to do something and you say that you're busy. Instead, just say that you have more important things to do, that it really doesn't interest you, or isn't a priority.

Maybe that sounds a bit harsh, but it's honest. If you did really want to do it you would find a way.

How are you using your time? What is your priority?

Money can always be made again. Time cannot. You can't buy back more time. It stands still for no one. It's life's most precious resource. Make time for what truly matters.

What Is Your Hourly Rate?

How do you handle the compulsion to say, "there isn't enough time" or "there aren't enough hours in the day"?

You can look at that from a couple different directions. The first is that it probably means you're doing too much and need to hire more people to help you. Certain duties need to be delegated to others.

The other is that you're probably a terrible manager

of your time. This is by far one of the most overlooked issues when evaluating your business and why you're overworked, underachieving, or not meeting the goals you set. It's not just for people that are in business or salespeople. This goes for everyone in their everyday, ordinary lives.

How do you manage your time? Are you planning tomorrow today? During your work hours are you solely focused on your goals or are you doing things that are counterproductive?

A great way to measure this is to look back at your past two days. Between the hours you allocate to work, say eight to four or nine to five, were you productive? What did you accomplish? Did the duties you completed get you closer to your goals?

Where is all your time going each day, week, and month? Write down all the activities and things that are eating up your time and not allowing you to achieve your priorities and goals. This shows you how your time is being spent.

Naval Ravikant shares a great tool to help with this problem. He said, "Set and enforce an aspirational hourly rate. If fixing a problem will save less than your rate, ignore it. If outsourcing a task will cost less than your rate, outsource it. Get comfortable disappointing people whose expectations will eat your life up, one hour at a time."

I've adopted this simple principle to help decide whether or not I should do something or delegate it. I set an hourly wage on my time. I use a simple $100 an hour. What's yours? Is it $25, $50, $100, or $250 an hour. As your time becomes more valuable this rate may increase. If I'm doing something that doesn't equal out to be worth $100 an hour, I will delegate it.

At $100 an hour, if I'm going to the post office to get stamps, going to the bank, taking payments, or billing clients, I'm not allocating my time properly. Hire people to take care of this stuff. You need to focus on what provides the most value to your business and team. Spending my time on something that someone else is qualified to do or can be trained to do is a waste. I need to focus on the responsibilities and priorities that only I can fulfill.

Think about what you can pay out to save you time. Give yourself the needed time for your priorities. Are your priorities matching your goals for your business? Are trips to the bank, post office, grocery store eating up your time? What about cleaning the office, lawn care and snow removal needs, or payroll, clerical, and accounting needs? Are there things you no longer want to do and you have the budget to hire people to do them? Can you potentially replace yourself at your business?

This is about speaking value into your priorities. It will also speak value into those you delegate responsibilities to. However, here's an important side note: the $100 an hour, or whichever amount you use, has nothing to do with the time spent with your family and kids. This is meant to reprioritize the relationships and tasks that matter most. Never use this measure for your family. That time is invaluable.

If you do this with your family activities, go talk to someone so you can kick this before it ruins your marriage or your relationship with your kids. I say this, and am very direct about it, because I have seen this ruin too many families. Work is important but family is more important.

I think of wealth now as being rich in time. Having the time to do what you want, when you want, and with whom you want. Obviously, there are other responsibilities in life that are away from the office. Can this principle apply to them? Absolutely!

Spending your money to better your life and the lives of those around you has lasting benefits. Saving time now may allow you to work out and improve your health. Saving time now can allow more time with your family. Saving time now opens up time to achieve a goal you've set for yourself.

I hate mowing the lawn. That one is easy. It takes up too much time in my week and I can't do anywhere near as well as a professional. Washing the windows, inside and out, would take me a whole Saturday on a rickety ladder. A pro can do it in an hour and a half and it'll only cost $150-$200 every three months or so.

Now, my wife loves to garden. The time she spends on it is rejuvenating. I don't understand it, but I'm not going to hire that out, because she and the kids really enjoy it. She also loves to cook, but that doesn't mean that on a rough day we won't order in.

Do you see where I'm going with this? There are some responsibilities that bring the family together and others that would cause us to be apart. I like to hire out as much as I can of the things that take away from time with my family. And, bonus, you're helping to support a local, small business.

There are a lot of things taking up our time. Outsource the things that take away from your priorities. You could:

- Order something online that will arrive in a few

days on your doorstep versus spending the time and cost of gas to drive somewhere to pick it up.

- Pay a landscaper to mulch in your landscape rather than doing it yourself. They'll probably do a much better job.
- Spend the money and the minutes it takes to go through the car wash versus all the time of washing it yourself.
- Hire a financial advisor instead of stressing and spending time handling all your own investments.
- Invest in index funds versus spending all the time researching investments.
- Hire an accountant to take care of your taxes instead of trying to tackle them on your own.
- Have food delivered instead of getting in your car and driving to go pick it up to then just bring it back home.

I could go on and on with examples. Everyone's list varies, but you get the point. Can you see how a change in your perspective can speak better value into your priorities?

How many of those activities do you hate doing and are taking up time? It's not always a return on investment. Think in terms of return on hassle. Adjust your line of thinking to reflect how much hassle this could cause. Now add your time on top of that. What's your time worth?

The next time you're considering if something is really worth your time, ask yourself, is this really worth it at "X" per hour? How much time is this activity taking away from me?

What's worth doing?

Eliminate the time-sucking things you hate doing. Find alternative ways to do them. Hire or outsource to a company, service, or others to do them for you.

If you could remove a certain activity that you hate doing, what is that worth to you?

Worth to you in time? Worth to you in reduced hassle? Worth to you in happiness? Worth to you so you can focus on your goals and priorities?

We have so much we want to do, but only so much time. There are only so many days to fit all of it in. So, we ask ourselves, where do we find the time for this and that? How are we going to fit this in? How do I find more time to spend with my family? How and what do I prioritize?

We all struggle with where to properly spend our time. We don't prioritize all the things we do. Is this thing you need to do worth the hassle? What's your time really worth? What's your hourly rate to determine if this or that is worth doing, when it takes you away from your priorities?

Prioritize the time in your life. We only have so much of it. Spend it on the things and with the people that are truly important to you.

Part 3
Gaining Perspective

13

The Story of Sam

Vacations are a funny thing. Regardless of where you go, whether you drive or fly, there is a sense of relaxation, but also some stress. Will we get there on time? Will our flights be delayed? Will our hotel and the other places have our reservations correct? It goes through everyone's mind on a vacation.

With kids along there is a bit more stress added instead of the relaxation part. In fact, it's more of an expedition than a vacation. You're taking care of your kids in a different city or state. It will usually reach a point where you can't wait to get home, but oh the fun and memories it provides along the way.

We took our kids on a trip to Chicago and the surrounding suburbs. They love the Home Alone movies, so we went and checked out the Home Alone house in Winnetka, IL. My wife and I also loved the movies, so it was fun for us all.

It's really cool to see in person. The entire time we were there, families were walking up constantly taking pictures of it.

We also made stops at the Chicago Botanical Gardens (breathtakingly beautiful), the renowned Geneva Art Show, Shedd Aquarium, Field Museum, and Navy Pier.

What do you think the kids remembered the most

and continue to talk about every day since? The Home Alone house? The dinosaurs and mummies at the Field Museum? All the live animals, sharks and whales at the Shedd Aquarium? The ferris wheel and rides at Navy Pier?

None of those were it.

It was a man named Sam.

Sam was the bellman at the Thompson Hotel in downtown Chicago.

This was the first place that we stayed on our trip. Sam took care of our vehicle and brought all our luggage up to our room upon arrival. No small feat, as you'd think we packed enough to be away for a month.

What stuck out was how genuine Sam was. He connected with our kids immediately.

Maybe it was the fact that he has kids himself.

Whenever we left the hotel he asked where we were headed and if we needed anything. If we went out to dinner, he asked where we were going. When we returned, he asked how it was. He'd get excited when he saw the kids. That excitement was shared by the kids.

No matter where we went, the kids asked if Sam would be there when we returned. As we pulled up they'd perk up whenever they saw him. They would get out and instantly run towards Sam. He would hug them. It was so cute to see.

In the mornings when we went out to go to breakfast though, Sam was never there. The kids were sad. Where is Sam? The sad faces would ensue. They couldn't see their friend.

It turns our Sam didn't start his days until 2:00.

Why did a young man with a young family start his

days at 2:00 and work late into the evenings? Because he likes to take his kids and see them off to school. He preferred that.

After four days, my kids at the ages of four and six bonded with a man they'd never met before.

It wasn't all the animals, rides, big buildings or fancy things they saw that made them happy. It was a man named Sam. A man who is just genuinely nice and cares enough to talk with a family from Wisconsin. To make their stay feel memorable and treat them like a part of his family. That's true hospitality.

He shared photos of his family. We took pictures on the last day. He and the kids even took some food and fed the birds and pigeons. It's the simplest things that result in smiles and memories.

We can all learn something from people like Sam. Being a genuine person who just wants to ask how you are, how your day was, how dinner was, is often overlooked. It's the little things we neglect. All of us would be so lucky to meet someone like Sam who operates in the kind and genuine manner that he does.

What type of impact does Sam have on the Thompson Hotel? Imagine all the people who come back as repeat guests just because of him. To be honest the beds at the Thompson Hotel were terrible. The beds were so short that our feet hung off the edge. Yes, I did share those thoughts with the hotel. It was annoying!

But do you think we will go back? Of course we will! We have to! When we left, that was the saddest part of the trip for the kids. They wondered when they would see Sam again. They hugged him, smiled, and waved as we hopped in the vehicle to drive off.

It was the end of their time with their friend Sam, but it wasn't the end of hearing his name and asking when we will see him again. That's all we've heard since we left.

There will come a time that we stay at the Thompson Hotel again because of Sam. When we arrive you can bet hugs will be shared with a bellman named Sam, who became a family friend.

14

Take Timeouts

After a hard stretch of work, I call a timeout for myself. I view it as setting aside time for myself. Is it selfish? Some could view it that way, but the only person it matters to is me, and I just do it. I'm convinced everyone should do it.

In my calendar, I have specific times that I set aside to slow down. I will do my yoga practice, usually twice a week for up to an hour. I schedule a haircut every two weeks, pedicure every four weeks, and a full body massage once a quarter.

The key to taking regularly scheduled time away, and making it as beneficial as possible, is to schedule the next immediately after you do it the first time. If you don't do it right away, you'll forget to schedule it. If it doesn't become consistently scheduled, you will go extended periods without it. I know, because I've done it.

How many people do you know, when telling them you're going to get a massage, will say, "oh I could really use one of those," or "I'm so jealous"? Well, when was the last time you went to get a massage or pedicure? Take the initiative. If you want to do something, make the time and set it in your schedule.

The same goes for vacations. My wife and I plan two vacations a year at a week minimum. In addition, we schedule a few separate getaways, for two or three days. These are the types of things you need to do to create a work, family, and life balance.

It gives you a perspective from outside your work environment. You're relaxed with your family and you see things you otherwise wouldn't.

The story about Sam never would have happened had we not taken a family vacation. The interaction with someone brought to light an unforgettable service experience. Just the interaction with someone who took work seriously, but was also very personable all while having fun was a lesson in itself. He valued what was important.

Traveling with kids, we're creating memories that they will remember forever. Vacations have become a ton of fun. It's not just the kids that get excited. My wife and I get just as excited.

I actually think my wife and I were more excited to take the kids to Disney World the first time. Just watching them made the trip for me. Memories last a lifetime. We try to make as many as possible.

Being Present

The biggest addiction we have in society today is our phones.

It has become so bad, that now we have watches that will notify us when our phone gets a call, text, email, or notification from one of the numerous apps we have. So if we aren't driving, walking, or sitting with it up to our face, the watches will now tell us to put it back up to our face.

We're always going to have constant distractions. Every company in the world is throwing their marketing at us at every turn. Our screens are filled with advertising and things to keep us watching or scrolling. Everyone is trying to balance work, their personal lives, and a fear of missing out. Our minds are worrying and constantly thinking about our to-do lists. It all prevents us from being fully present in the here and now.

Work, what I had to do the next day, and whatever else was running through my mind was preventing me from being fully present at times in my life. It turned out my wife was asking me if I remembered her telling me this and that? I wasn't remembering it.

At first I laughed about it and shrugged it off. We've all heard it, a husband not listening to his wife. Sadly, I wasn't even aware that I was not paying attention to our conversations. I realized I was there, but wasn't fully present and listening. At times I must have seemed like a zombie.

I'd recall the conversations, but not what was really said. I wasn't fully focused and my attention was elsewhere. I wasn't listening. It was a bit embarrassing and I needed to improve it. So I made steps to fix it.

Out of the room went my phone, especially at dinner time. I had to create separation from it. Eliminating the distraction altogether was very important. It sounds easy to do, but I know friends who really struggle with this. It's a hard addiction to break and takes time.

At a certain time in the evening, and before bed, we turn off the TV and electronic devices. This is very important not just for kids, but also for adults.

Prioritize conversation. Talk with your family. Play games and have some interaction.

Phones, TVs, and electronic devices isolate yourself

to the screen. Then test yourself. At the end of the day, ask yourself the following;

- What did we eat and discuss at breakfast, lunch, or dinner?
- What do you remember about the conversations with your spouse and kids?
- What funny or goofy thing did the kids do that made everyone laugh?

If you're not instantly remembering, then you're in zombie mode. Wake up and snap out of it. Turn off distractions. Be present and in the moment. Pay attention, participate and connect. Get off autopilot.

Tim Urban laid out the human lifespan visually in his blog post, *The Tail End*. This post had a profound impact on me. I think about it often. Take a moment and read the entire post.

Below are two parts that have stuck with me.

"No matter what your age, you may, without realizing it, be enjoying the very last chapter of the relationships that matter most to you. Make it count."

"It turns out that when I graduated from high school, I had already used up 93% of my in-person parent time. I'm now enjoying the last 5% of that time. We're in the tail end."

Contrary to what everyone would like to do, we can't slow down time. The clock ticks and will always continue to tick. Call or go see your parents, grandparents, and kids. Time is shorter than you think.

The competition for our time is fierce. Everyone is fighting for it. Who gets your undivided attention is up to you. Don't make your kids or family compete for it too.

Make Time For What Matters

As I sat on the patio at my favorite coffee shop one afternoon, I realized that the hour I'd just spent at lunch was an appointment with social media.

After sitting for an hour, only 10 minutes of that time was spent eating, the rest was spent mindlessly scrolling. *What a complete waste of time*, I thought to myself.

That's 17% of the time eating and the other 73% of it wasted. I may as well have flushed that time down the toilet. I'm not getting it back. Money you can always make back, time you can't. I can go to a bank and get loans for money. You can't do that with time.

So, I started reevaluating where all my time was being spent throughout my days and weeks. I realized social media was a massive time drain. It was hours a day and I was getting nothing from it.

Same as watching TV. Instead of watching a three-hour movie I was looking at my phone for three hours a day on social media sites. Instead of having to be confined to my couch to watch a movie, I could watch it on the go no matter where I was on my phone.

That's what I was doing with social media; wasting away hours of my life. My busyness was scrolling through news feeds and continually hitting refresh, needing that dopamine hit. It was an addiction.

Most complain about it, then stay on because they're addicted to it. They don't think they could survive without it, like it would create a massive void in their life that they could never replace. The fear of missing out sets in.

At the beginning of each year, I look at how to realign my schedule to what is most important and of highest priority. I want to find more time to write, think, and investigate new ideas. I want to spend more time with my kids and leave work earlier with all my to-dos done.

When I looked over my appointments and events in my calendar, I could see time being spent on things that weren't important. They weren't things that I wanted to do. Why did I even say yes to them in the first place? It was time to reevaluate where and how I spent my time. Not just free time, but all my time.

I started to ask myself, "Is this worth my time? Is this going to benefit me or my family? Will this help allow me to reach my goals in life?" If the answer to any of these questions was no, then it didn't make it onto my calendar. It was time to reorganize and reprioritize.

Jim Collins says it this way, "If you had ten years to live, what would you stop doing?"

My goal was ultimately to drain the swamp of wasted time. Time-wasting on social media was gone. The meetings that provided no value were gone. Duties at the office that didn't need me were gone. I had teammates I could delegate work to. I could hire out for it. Going to the post office, dropping off packages, going to the bank, going to the dry cleaner, and mowing the lawn were all delegated.

In unplugging social media, as I said earlier, I freed up hours a day. What would you do with a few extra hours a day? All of this helped me to zero-in on what matters most to me.

Do What Makes You Happy

I drive twenty miles every morning to get coffee. Why? Because I want to go to my favorite place that has the best coffee. Our favorite restaurant is over an hour away. If we're going out to dinner we usually go there. Why? Because they have the best food. There is a reason athletes and celebrities go there. Go and enjoy the best. Life is too short to eat shitty food.

You got a great deal on a steak. Big deal! Remember the cheaper the cut, the lower the quality of meat it is. You get what you pay for! Pay up and have one of the best steaks and dinners of your life!

Too many people judge people for doing the things that make them happy. Who cares!

It's their time and money. Worry about yourself and not what others are doing.

Why sacrifice quality when you can go have your favorite? The career you pick is the same. Make sure the job you're going to daily is the best. Make sure you absolutely love it!

I can't wait to go get coffee each morning from my favorite coffee place. When I know we're going to dinner, I am jacked for days before we go. Is that weird? Maybe, but when you love something that much you have a totally different outlook.

When I wake up, I view my job the same. I can't wait to get into the office. Do you have things that make you feel that way? Do them! Don't wait! Remember, life is too short to eat shitty food. Life is too short to write with a shitty pen. Life is too short to have a shitty job. Life is too short to drink shitty coffee. I think you get the idea. Now, get doing things and going places that excite you.

If a massage makes you feel like a million bucks, then set them up. Allow yourself to do what you love and makes you happy. Don't do things to satisfy the demand that other's put on you. Your loved ones are the obvious exception. Maintain a good balance of taking care of others and yourself. It can be easy to neglect what you need. Doing things you enjoy helps you to feel refreshed and happy. The question to ask yourself is when was the last time you looked forward to doing something?

Have a Bucket List

Have you ever made a list of what you want to accomplish, where you want to go, and what you want to do in this life? Do you have a list like that? Many refer to this as their bucket list, but it often gets neglected.

Why do people have to be told they have cancer before they make a bucket list and take that trip? Shouldn't you work on that list your whole life, starting it while you're young?

Whatever you do, don't wait or rely on retirement to do these things. There are way too many variables, and the odds are not in your favor. You're going to be older. Will you be healthy?

Everything will only get more expensive the longer you wait. The value of money will be less. If you have kids, they'll be older and have their own families. They may not be able to go with you. If you can do it now, do it.

That two-week trip to Italy costs, let's say, $10,000. You just went on a trip with your kids that they'll remember forever, because you're all at ages that you can go and enjoy it together. You can see and do much more. By waiting you're ensuring that it costs more in the future.

Now go when you're 70. Can you walk? How much will you be able to see? Your children are unable to go because they just had another baby. Quit making excuses. Live your best life now!

Aim to achieve your dreams and goals. Move through life making your bucket list something you look to accomplish next month, this year, or the next. Don't aim to do these in ten years, twenty years, or, worse yet, retirement.

Many will say one thing but do another. We sleepwalk and just go through the motions day by day. Having goals or aspirations make your path clearer. Your eyes get widened to see the whole picture.

We put off making changes, chasing dreams, or obtaining goals because of uncertainty.

The question to ask yourself is, "why am I waiting?" We wait out of the fear of being judged for what we do. We wait for the timing to be perfect. We wait for a stamp of approval, or the assurance that things will work out and be fine. Often, life gets more uncertain, so we continue to wait longer.

The truth is, we're always going to be judged, the timing will never be perfect, hard decisions never feel good, and the only stamp of approval that matters is your own.

I waited too many years to start my blog, *Spilled Coffee*. I waited too long to write this book. And for what? I accomplished nothing by waiting. So, why did I wait? All of the likely reasons: fear of uncertainty and the unknown, of criticism and being judged, and a fear of failure one of my biggest regrets is that I didn't write sooner. How many times do we hear others say they wish they had done something sooner? Do you ever hear, I wish I had waited longer?

In this current moment you know the variables. You know the risks, the positives and negatives. In waiting, you add an element of time that brings with it unknown variables, for better or worse. The future is totally unknown. We have no idea what the future months and years will bring.

Waiting for a stamp of approval? I'll stamp it! Perfect timing? The perfect timing is now. Take the leap. Don't wait like I did. The pandemic of 2020 taught our society that we shouldn't wait any longer to achieve our dreams. You are not guaranteed tomorrow, so live accordingly.

15
Perspective

You might be wondering why I've dedicated a part of my book to time off and time well spent. Time away lends a perspective that you don't see while you're at work.

My family's time in Chicago introduced us to Sam, whose work was fueled by passion and care that touched my family deeply. He reminded me that how we treat people matters. That, in turn, gave me ideas and taught me how to better run my business. It showed how we interact with people matters. How you are as a person matters.

In a world that is becoming less and less people focused and more focused on automation, this is important. With less companies speaking in person or physically seeing their customers, showing personality, communication in person, and kindness stand the test of time. It never gets old. It's irreplaceable and unable to be duplicated. You can't replace those human elements.

It made me realize that interaction with people genuinely matters. Telling and creating stories has an impact. Being genuine and personable sprouts meaningful interaction. Caring, showing empathy, being helpful, all means more to people than I think we realize. You never know where it may lead or what type of thoughts it may spur. There is an impact that helps you grow professionally and personally.

Getting out and away from work offers these perspectives. It allows you to stop bushwhacking your way through and instead allows you to see the forest through the trees. You get out of the valley and onto the mountain top to see where you're going.

Some of my best ideas came alongside a fresh perspective. Whether it was an interaction with someone that taught me something I'd never considered, visiting a place I'd like to visit more often, or just because I was a newbie in the industry, getting out of the day-to-day from time to time will help in unforeseen ways. Fresh perspective helps gear your business to the greatest gain, and that doesn't always mean money.

Take time to unwind. Take that vacation you've been wanting to take. It's why you work so hard after all. You may even come across your own Sam who helps give you a fresh perspective on your life.

Part 4
Reaching People You Want

16

The Magic Letter

February is the slowest month in the insurance business. It's also one of the worst months when you live in Wisconsin. There is nothing going on in February other than winter.

In February of 2005, I was looking for new ways to market to homeowners and find some new clients. I spent multiple nights working on a letter to send prospective clients. How can I grab someone's attention? I'd asked myself. I wanted to target the large homes around Green Lake, Wisconsin.

Green Lake is a beautiful place. The majority of homeowners are from Chicago, and most homes on the lake are five to fifteen thousand square feet, so they're more mansions than homes.

I wanted to target the homes of the executives and CEOs of major companies, hoping to just land a few or just make contact with some of the residents. Being 20 years old at the time, any conversations or connections that I could gain from this would be worth it.

One of the homes I wanted to target I'd been able to spend some time in when I was younger. I helped my dad while he was doing the plumbing in this massive mansion referred to as the Walgreens Home.

It turned out to be the lake home for L. Daniel Jorndt, the CEO of Walgreens. This home has 13 bathrooms and 11 bedrooms. Pretty cool when every bedroom has a bathroom attached to it. It's still my favorite home on the entire lake.

I thought about how I could word a letter to Dan to get him to reply to me, but what the heck do you write to someone that runs one of the best companies in the world?

When I started in sales, I had always heard the myth of the magic letter, a letter that would guarantee a reply and sale. The joke was that the magic letter was locked up in a vault. If it's in a vault, then don't plan on being able to crack the code. Instead, try and discover your own magic letter.

To create one of my own, there were three things that I needed to figure out. First, what would make the prospective client open the letter? Then, what would make them read what I had to say? Lastly, what would make them take action? This letter needed to stand out and be as personal as I could make it.

After a few weeks of spending seemingly endless hours, I had it all together.

I got a list of homeowners around Green Lake. On that listing it showed the address of the home and the homeowner's mailing address. Many of the homes I was going after were high end exclusive lake homes. In our area that meant that many of these customers did not live there full time.

On the front of the envelope, I hand wrote their name and address. On the bottom of the letter there was some extra space, so on each I'd write a little handwritten note. I enclosed an orange reply form and a self-addressed envelope.

I made the handwritten note as personalized as I could. If I had worked on this home or a home nearby during the days that I had worked with my Dad, I told them. If I painted that home or their neighbor's, I told them. Some of these homes I had been to while owned by someone prior to them.

The goal was to make it as personal as I could. Almost like we knew each other, but never met. Sounds kind of corny, but that's the approach I took.

I recall wondering at one point, if it's even worth my time. People will probably just throw it out. Odds are these people have someone else take care of their mail. They probably don't even see it.

The hell with it, I thought. What could it hurt? What happened after I mailed those letters made a lifelong impact on me.

It took a little over a week, and to my surprise, they were responding. Many were "no, but thank you for the nice letter." I was amazed how many people hand wrote a note back. Many had long established relationships with other insurance agents or companies, but they took the time to write that to me. It was like we were pen pals.

Not all said no though. In fact, many said yes! I had people emailing and calling me in addition to mailing back the orange form. It seemed I had discovered something. My schedule started to book up. I needed to meet many on the weekends as these were their seasonal homes and they would only be up on the weekends. I was 20 years old, so I didn't care. I was insuring multimillion-dollar homes and helping handle all their insurance needs. Some even brought me their primary homes in other cities and states many of the first responders to this letter are still clients of mine today. In all my years in business this is still the best response I have ever had from a letter.

My end goal was to stand out to them as a trusted advisor, but also someone that had a good product to sell them. I believe what really made me stand out was with the personalization in the handwritten note. The handwritten address just helped in making them open the letter, but that personalized note really made this a magic letter.

They Replied!

The magic letter provided two memorable experiences that have forever changed my life.

Later that month I received a call. It was the owner of one the largest and most beautiful pieces of property on the entire lake in my opinion. He was coming up that weekend with his family and wanted to meet me.

So, early on a Saturday morning we met at his awe-inspiring property. We sat on the patio to one of the most beautiful sunrises I've ever witnessed.

We spoke about what drew his attention to my letter. As a young kid, my dad, uncle, and I would ice-fish off this property. My uncle knew the prior owners so every winter we would fish together from a large shack on the shoreline.

We'd sled down the hill in the snow and enjoy the various snow and ice activities throughout the winter. It was surreal to relive those moments while I sat there looking at the hill and shoreline that gave all those memories.

During those two hours we spent together we spent about ten minutes talking insurance. The rest of the time we just talked about a little of everything. Sports, life, money, wealth, and anything else we could cram in for two hours. We could have sat and talked longer, but his wife and child were up now and ready to get on with their day. I did take care of his insurance and to this day he is still one of my clients.

We periodically have our talks, but he hardly ever makes it back to that home of his anymore. We resort to phone calls and emails now, but the impact and confidence I had gained after that conversation on the patio was immeasurable. I had an entire mindset shift.

The second memorable response didn't come until March 18th, a Thursday afternoon. I had an email pop into my inbox from Dan Jorndt, the CEO of Walgreens. The house I had targeted and the entire reason for trying to write a magic letter.

First thing I thought was, "Holy shit! He received and must have read my letter!"

When I was a kid, I remember going into that house because my Dad was doing the plumbing on it. It was a massive mansion. The home that many dream of just being able to go into one day.

While putting his letter together, I noted that. I explained to him that I was in this home as child and would love to show him what I had to offer. I was brutally honest. I wanted to sit and speak with him about business and life. What made him what he is today. I wanted to learn from him, not just handle his insurance.

At the time, Walgreens was one of the most admired and successful companies. Being a 20-year-old kid living in a city with a population of 1,200 people, this may be the only chance I get to meet someone with this status or influence. What resulted was something that I never would have expected.

When I opened the email, it turned out to be rather long. It touched on all aspects of life and business. He openly shared his tips and lessons that he had learned during his fifty years as a retailer. Then listed how to apply them to life and business. It was truly invaluable advice for a young kid just starting his career.

Many of these things have become a playbook for me. I've tried to do the best I could to take what he told me as pillars upon which to build my success both personally and professionally. Here are some things that really stuck out to me:

"Remember, too, that money isn't everything."

"Keep learning—try things, watch, read, listen. Stay interested and you'll stay interesting."

"Tell the truth, be ethical. Do what's right for the customer." "Set high goals for you and your team."

"Be audacious, take risks."

"Build your business and it is your business."

"Invest your time, your energy, your money. $200 bucks a month, earning 10%=$1.3 million after 40 years"

Was this a magic letter? To me it sure was! The magic, however, wasn't the sale and business that it brought. It was in the lessons these men had learned that they then shared with me.

One became a client and the other didn't. It taught me that not everything comes down to money. In life, there are more things that you can gain than just money. It turned out, making a sale and making money wasn't necessary to achieve a win.

I told a story and was personal with them both. That resulted in lessons about life that will stick with me forever. Lessons from people that most never get the opportunity to talk to about these things.

What I thought was all about money and selling wasn't what I had learned. It was about spending time with family and friends. It was about saying thank you, and saying it to everyone. Treating teammates and co-workers the way I'd want to be treated. I learned to not worry about work too much. We all need to take time away from work to relax and refresh. It helps us to see things clearer. Success in something doesn't always translate to money.

17

Selling Certainty

Why isn't everyone cut out for sales? It's a good question. Since everyone is wired differently, I don't think there is a blanket answer for this.

I believe that a main reason is the instant reaction of fear and uncertainty. When you look at sales whether you're selling insurance, financial planning advice, electronics, or whatever it may be, you're really trying to sell certainty.

Whatever you're selling, you're trying to convey it's the best. It will last the longest or work when it's needed most. Hopefully, the product actually is the best when you tell people it is.

People always want certainty. It's how we are as humans. Why are repeat customers such easy sales? It's because they have already bought from you or already purchased your product or service in the past. They have certainty with what they're buying.

Consider the uncertainty from the prospective client's side of things. What is this person trying to sell me? Do I have this product already? Have I bought from this person before? Have I ever bought anything from this company before? If this person is not a repeat customer, the answer to all these questions is no.

As a salesperson, the fear of making that unsolicited phone call or email to someone is creating uncertainty for the salesperson. You're replaying in your head the hundreds of different objections the prospect could have. It could result in a no, could result in a maybe, or they will just say yes! We hate being told no and experiencing rejection.

Add to all of this the cold call. Will they even need what I offer? Can they afford it? I don't know who's on the other end of the phone, it could be anyone. Just know, the more certain you are as a salesperson, the more certainty you can sell.

18
Who Is Your Customer?

Has anyone ever asked you who your customer is? If so, what has been your response?

Years ago, when I was helping out a new business owner in Oregon, he asked me, "Who is your customer? Who do you market to?"

"Well, everyone," I said.

I continued to advise and help him with some challenges he was having. After a conversation over two hours long, I hung up and began to reflect on that question he asked me. Who is my customer?

You never know when you'll learn something or who you will learn it from.

The reason he asked me that question is because I was giving him some help and ideas on marketing and targeting certain demographics. However, I realized that I wasn't really doing a deep enough targeted marketing program. I was trying to appeal to much too large a market and knew we could do better.

Sales people and business owners will often say that everyone is their customer. That just isn't true. Your product may be available to everyone and anyone can purchase it, but every business has its certain market or demographic it appeals to and sells the most to.

Focusing your time, energy, and money in the wrong places can have consequences. It distracts your focus away from the right places. The same goes for not having any focus.

It took me a few years to fully understand this, but I'm grateful for that conversation, and I've since then introduced some tools to help bring a much needed focus.

The Pareto Principle, named after economist Vilfredo Pareto, specifies that 80% of consequences come from 20% of the causes, asserting an unequal relationship between inputs and outputs. This is also known as the 80/20 principle.

It is the subject of a great book entitled *The 80/20 Principle: The Secret to Achieving More with Less* by Richard Koch. He does a masterful job detailing how this can be applied practically to life, career, and business.

Applying it to your business can clearly illustrate where your productivity, time, and money should be spent. I used this principle to review past sales, revenues, and the makeup of my current client base. What could applying the principles tell me about how to identify the type of customers I wanted?

- 80% of the work we accomplish comes from 20% of the time
- 80% of our time is spent on 20% of our clients
- 80% of our revenue comes from 20% of our clients
- 80% of our sales are made by 20% of the sales team
- 80% of sales are produced by 20% of a company's product or service

As you can see, the 20% is the key. Identifying that

20% and building off of that will give you the insight you need to make the proper decisions moving forward. Two of the principles that stood out the most to me were that 80% of our complaints, problems, and time are spent on 20% of our clients, and 80% of our revenue comes from 20% of our clients.

I applied this to all aspects of my business: marketing, current clients, products, projects, sales, and service teams. Once I've identified 20% of my best customers—which I labeled the "A clients"—I could formulate a plan to focus on them. I needed to market to the "A clients" and be sure they were getting the best service, advice, and experience possible.

By applying these principles, I also realized that we were going to have to give up some "C" clients to provide better commitment and attention to an "A" client. The 80% of problems, complaints, and time that 20% of our clients caused was not worth our time. It was taking our time away from our best clients. It wasn't fair to either of them.

You can't be everything to everyone if you want to offer a truly exceptional experience.

Certain clients do not fit. Always remember, quality of business over quantity of business.

Is Your Brand Speaking to the Clients You Want?

If you've applied the 80/20 principle to your business and now identified your "A" clients, it's time to customize your brand to speak to them.

Identifying the proper customer segment for your marketing is vital. This will allow you to stand out and be remembered by those prospective clients.

I'd already realized how much I'd steered my company toward a market-to-everyone mentality, but I was curious what impression we had left. It was evident. We weren't targeting anyone. We noticed it was a shotgun approach. We needed to rifle in on our intended targets.

To do this we needed to run research on what qualities made up the clients we wanted. Due to account size, revenue, margins, and retention we knew they needed to be married and homeowners. Then, homeowners owning above a certain value of home in specific zip codes. Target down to the street. Get picky and then stand out. Wow them!

It soon became clear that this not only affected who we market to, but also how we communicate. After evaluating this we knew we needed to adjust our mission statement and change our introduction when people visited our website. We changed it to read the following.

Wisconsin Agency of the Year - Custom Crafted
Insurance Policies

Our goal is to provide distinctly customized insurance policies with an emphasis on developing long term personal client relationships. We are a nationally awarded team of professionals dedicated to helping you. Through this personalized approach, our agency has grown to be one of the largest American Family agencies in the country. Let our family protect your family.

We had to make ourselves stand out and tell people we're the best. Why? Because we needed to grab them

132

right away, and make them say to themselves this is an agency we want to work with. They must be the best.

I asked myself, "How would I want to be talked to? What would I want to see and read? What would wow me?"

Be sure that the message you're trying to convey matches who you are and who you are talking to. If you want every Tom, Dick and Harry, then have a bland, boring, generic message that speaks to everyone. Just know, you'll also compete with all the other businesses like yours. You'll blend in. Do you know what happens when you do that? You speak to no one.

Focus! Zero in. Ask yourself what your ideal client is. Make a list of the qualities they have. Do you want to be viewed as general or affordable? Or, do you want to be known as the expert and exclusive advisor. The best!

Then determine what you need to do to reach that clientele. Make sure your website and social media all have the same consistent message. Does that message stand out? Are you being unique and different?

Be sure to build off that branding. Carry it over to your TV commercials, billboards, and any direct mail marketing you do. All your advertising and marketing needs to speak to the same message and to the right prospective client.

We have identified the traits and demographics of our ideal client. Our agency branding, mission statement, and message all comes from there.

Who is our target market? Homeowners valued in a certain dollar range. What is our message? That we specialize in custom crafted homeowner's insurance policies.

19
Finding Your Ideal Clients

Part of what went into creating an experience for our clients was engineering a plan to attract and retain the best client. So, what do you look for in your ideal client? Here are the traits that we looked for:

- Clients who were good payers
- Clients who would take the time to review their products when we advised it.
- Clients who maintain good loss ratios and are a good risk. In the insurance business that means clients who were not always filing claims.
- Clients who paid us above a certain amount in premium per year.
- Clients who value personalized advice and time we would spend with them.
- Clients who won't constantly try to pressure us to lower their insurance premiums.

What does that customer segment look like? This is where you use your data to design how you want to market to this group of people. Ways to customize and speak to this group by marital status, age bracket, industry and occupation, location, income level, education, home value, and so on.

Identify your targeted customer demographics and speak to them through your marketing and advertising.

You will not stand out to anyone if you try to appeal to everyone.

Out of our existing book of business this group of clients was very easy to identify. As I detailed earlier, we did develop personalized service plans for these clients. We really wanted to take care and retain the clients that checked those boxes.

The hard part came in trying to find more of these people to become our clients. Where do you begin? How do you convince this type of clientele to trust you? I hope to save you years of pounding your head against the wall!

The first thing I did was try to research and see what others have done to conquer this question. A couple books that I read in addition to the 80/20 principle were: *Giftology* by John Ruhlin, *No B.S. Marketing to the Affluent* by Dan Kennedy, *No B.S. Trust-Based Marketing* by Dan Kennedy & Matt Zagula, and *Never Lose a Customer Again* by Joey Coleman.

These books really cover all the aspects you will want in how to best serve your clients, and how to find new ones. I've read many books on these subjects and I feel these four provided the most help.

An essay I read that really helped was *1,000 True Fans* by Kevin Kelly. Read and study what he says. Then, try to relate it to your business. It's really eye opening.

Prospective Client Marketing Program

Now that we knew who we wanted to market to, the objective was to design ways to try and stand out to them. To get them to contact us and to be the first people they think of when they think of their insurance.

Many businesses think, "I will just advertise on everything and everywhere." But what you do is flush a lot of money down the drain.

If you get customers, but your margins are terrible, then your cost of acquiring customers is too high. Therefore, identifying the client you want, allows you to go after those certain qualities.

When I tell people the little amount of money we spend on marketing, many are stunned.

What I do spend time and energy on is identify the best ways to directly target my preferred audience. My marketing is rather simple, a 6-part program:

- Billboards
- Direct Mail Program
- Internet Presence and Social Media
- Water
- Hot List
- Winning Back Old Clients

For all of these six programs I ask myself and my team two simple questions: 1.) Who is our target market? 2.) What is our message?

I want everything to remain simple and easy for me and my team. If they're asking questions and I don't know the answer, then I know I made it too complicated. The same goes for our clients. We want our clients and prospective clients to be able to do business with us simply and easily. If not, they will go with someone else. The easier we make it for the team translates to the customer. Creating and fitting a program to what you want is well worth the time.

Who is your target market? What is your message?

These two questions can cut out many other forms of marketing. If you can't zero in on a target message and communicate it, then that advertising is not for you and your business.

Consistency is key. Our message should be consistent. Where and how we market should be consistent. Develop your marketing plan, then, establish what forms of advertising you can do. Do not spread your dollars and time too thin. Start with a couple and master those before you expand.

It took many years for us to reach six different programs. When I began I had two programs. Then, went to three. Take baby steps. Be sure you're giving your program time to work. Make certain you are properly measuring results.

Do something different. Try something nobody else has. See what happens. Remember, by going with the crowd, you blend in with the crowd. To stand out, you need to separate and be different.

Billboards

The public knowing that your business exists is one of the most important steps in starting your business. What do I provide that can help you? Then, how do I convey that message across to a wide audience? What large scale marketing program will reach the larger audience?

We had looked at and tried many different marketing ideas. The one we discovered, and have stuck to my entire career, has been billboards. Yes, not the cheapest, but the impact that is provided is at a scale that nothing else can do for anything near the cost.

Return on investment and the awareness it provides stands alone.

The one program that can possibly do better is TV, but the cost and wide array of options never appealed to us. Between the numerous hours spent with TV sales execs and talking to others that have tried it, we'd keep coming back to the same conclusion. No thanks.

Since my second year in business, billboards have been a part of our marketing plan. We're able to change our message monthly if we want. Our billboard location changes every month. It's always on the move and usually with a fresh message.

If billboards are too expensive, find another business that could also benefit by sharing the billboard with you. If it's a business that you would want to be associated with, do it. This cuts your cost in half and may allow you to get your message up in a location that was otherwise unavailable to you.

So, what did our billboards say? Our message stays the same, but the way we communicate it changes all the time. It helps to give fresh perspective. Many times, they don't say much. We just emphasized a few words. If someone is driving, they only have a split second to look at and hopefully an impression was made in their mind.

Get your message across quickly and be sure a contact method is as clear and simple as possible. Usually, a website with the same name as your business will do that. Or, make your business name recognizable and easy to remember when they open their web browser to search it.

Our agency logo would always be quite large. The

message would appear short, usually only a few words or one sentence. Then our contact method was our website, ericsoda.com.

Of all the billboards we did, our most successful were when I decided to place the faces of my entire team. We received compliments from existing clients, past clients, and people we had never met before.

The feedback commended me for highlighting my team. Around the community, people thought that it was just a cool and very nice thing to do for my teammates. They got comments from their friends and family about seeing them on a billboard. It really made them feel special.

When I'd thought of the idea, it just felt like a great thing to do. They work their butts off for me and my business, why wouldn't I highlight them. Why don't businesses do that? They are the powerhouses that keep the whole thing running.

It's that way in any business with employees. I can give a thank you and show that you really matter along with a marketing spin on it. I'm so glad I did it.

Is your team too big to fit? Consider running agency campaigns where the winners get to go up on the billboard.

The faces billboard drove new clients our way, made community statements where we ran them and gave a sense of great appreciation to my team. I'll be hard pressed to ever make a better marketing decision than this one.

Direct Mail Program

How much worthless junk mail do you get a day in

your mailbox? How much do you toss without even opening? You don't give it the time of day because it looks like a waste. It's impersonal and screams "throw me away!"

Now what about those direct mail pieces that catch your eye? The ones that you open and think, "oh, that was a nice message." What color scheme or pictures drew you in? Keep them.

Take a picture and put it in your marketing file.

I've kept a lot of eye-catching mail. Then, when I put together my mailers, I would use what worked on me. Keep what worked on you. Use it to your advantage when building your marketing material. You want it to be opened, so create a wow moment.

Be sure, whatever you do, to set a manageable cost. When you start, plan on doing this every quarter, then, as the budget allows, go monthly.

Don't be afraid to try handwritten addresses with a handwritten message inside. Hire a college or high schooler to help. Maybe hire a part time marketing person to help scale this.

People like the personal touch and it produces sales.

Consumers like to feel important. When you set up your target marketing program make sure you personalize it. It'll stand out.

The most mailed items we've used for direct mail have been postcards. Prospective clients get your message just by looking at them. They have to physically open a letter.

I find myself partially reading or at least glancing at the postcards I get. You can usually tell if it's advertising if it's an envelope. Those go right in the garbage. The most you see is the return address of the company or company logo.

Our postcards would always mirror what we had on our billboards around the area. If they saw our billboards, they would also get hit in the face with the postcard image as well. If they did turn it over, we would have some information and a simple message on the other side. Remember to have an eye-catching image on one side.

If you change your billboards or messages on other marketing material, be sure to change the postcard as well. Try to be consistent with the message across all your marketing.

Like any direct mail piece, you have to maintain consistent mailing. If your pieces are successful, you'll know.

Internet Presence and Social Media

Do you remember phone books? You used to be able to look in a phone book for the answer to all your questions. Now, they don't exist. Every business had to verify their information so that it was accurate in the phone book. You could pay for advertisements to make your brand stand out. Not too different nowadays. Except that phone books don't exist.

Now, we have the internet. To think your business doesn't need an internet presence in today's world is crazy. In my opinion, your website is the most important part. Social media platforms, much like the phone book, come and go. Fads change. What is the best platform now, soon won't be. A website keeps your most important information in a place that's the most accessible, no login or username required.

When starting out, after I made sure I had my website up and running properly, the next thing I did was set up internet leads. Yes, people do complete insurance quote requests from all those banners and ads that you see on websites. Actually, many more than you'd think.

Other industries also find prospective clients via ads promoting an action on the internet.

It's all about having multiple sales pipelines streaming into your business.

Early in my career, there wasn't a lot of competition with online insurance sales. Over the years as you have seen by the onslaught of advertising, insurance is now mainly pushed online. The competition increased, so I had to adapt our message and strategy.

Now when we get an internet lead there may be as many as ten other companies also contacting that prospective client. With the way insurance is advertised many people are just looking for the cheapest company. That isn't where we thrive, nor is that a targeted customer of ours.

Odds are you will not be the cheapest. If you are, good luck, because if you get their business due to being the cheapest, they will be the first to leave when you have a rate increase. Insurance companies always have increases, and the same is true of other types of businesses.

Instead of being the cheapest, sell yourself and your company on being the trusted advisor. Tell them to check out your website and look over what you offer, review your team, which is filled with many years of knowledge and experience. If they don't want advice or have a conversation, then they're just looking for the cheapest price, move on.

Many agencies do not have the capacity to handle internet leads. They take a lot of time.

Not all leads are valid or are real people looking for a quote. You have to sort through them.

If ten other companies are also calling and emailing the same prospective client, how do you stand out? You need to set the expectation. So, sell your clients on what you want to sell them on, yourself and your firm.

We don't pay for advertising on search engines, and Search Engine Optimization is a book in itself. Now, I am not an expert, so this is just how I look at it: The key with all the major search engines is to have reviews.

We uploaded pictures under our business profile. Made sure all our information was right. Then, we ask our clients to leave a review about our business. We have held a score of 4.9 out of 5 on Google. How do I know if it's working? We consistently ask new clients how they found us and Google is near the top.

In addition, I tasked our team to search various keywords as if they're searching for insurance, using whatever combination that they could think of to make sure we're on the top of the list. Do this for your business. If it's not showing up or you're not as easily discoverable when someone is searching for your type of business, then you have some work to do.

I don't know about you, but if I'm searching for new restaurants or places to go for certain things, I will check out their Google rating and number of reviews.

If you search for your business what are you going to find? Would you want to contact your business based on your rating and reviews?

Now, for the most powerful tool for business in the modern world: social media. It was not that many years ago that small businesses didn't even have an online presence and advertising on the internet didn't even exist. How fast things have changed.

This has become the most important and, for many businesses, the only way they operate. Social media has transformed how every industry and business operate today, and has become an endless sea of opportunities.

Each platform has its own objective, and has benefits and drawbacks. It's important to find which is best for your business. It's best not to get too tied to a single social media platform. They seem to go through cycles on which social media company is the preferred one. Make sure you're not tying your entire internet presence and company to a single platform.

Many people view your company's social media as the most up to date place to get information on your business. So, it needs to constantly be updated.

Most platforms allow you to increase the visibility of posts and turn them into ads that can catch a wide variety of consumers, even allowing you to zero in on your target customer, specific interests and keywords, and the geographical location by city and zip code. It has become one of the best values you can find for advertising.

As we make posts, we will then boost them and make an advertisement out of it for very little money. If we want to make it customized to a certain community, we can do so. It allows you to speak to certain groups very easily. Point, click, position and post. It's so simple. You just need to determine what you want to post.

Water

You're probably wondering why there is a section about water. Trust me, I didn't ever expect water to have the impact it did.

When we were pitched on the idea of agency branded water, I thought, "Well it's different, let's give it a try." Plus nobody else was doing it.

What we discovered was that nonprofit organizations and schools had to pay for the water that they sold at their events. They made very little money on it. We thought, why not donate pallets and cases of bottled water. What it cost was nothing compared to the amount it would help the local sports and recreational organizations. They rely on fundraising to be able to operate the local events and teams. This provided us a great way to give back.

We donated agency branded water bottles by the pallet load to various schools and organizations in our area. They were then able to turn around, sell that water and make money for their organizations.

Our agency receives many shout outs via social media and many nice cards thanking us for our generosity. It was nice to see clients and non-clients comment about our nice gesture of donating water.

They made up a nice agency branded logo and put it on natural spring water bottles. When we go to local events it's surreal to see our water bottles all over the place. This was something that made our entire team proud.

A number of clients over the years have commented on seeing our water bottles.

Everyone sees them. That combined with the generosity to our local communities makes an investment like this well worth it.

Hot List

On a cold winter evening in December of 2008, I put together what would become my single greatest agency program invention.

I was sick and tired of juggling when to follow up with clients as their renewal dates on their insurance policies were coming up. Many of these people were prospective clients I had spoken to in the past, but for various reasons decided against insuring with my firm.

There had to be an easier way. A way in which we can automate this better so I can have others on my team work this program. Something we can scale and fill with thousands of people.

I developed a simple spreadsheet. Their name, how we communicated, phone, and email could all go in there. I could then sort by their expiration date or date they wanted to be contacted. Then we could work that list in date order. Each month is a different tab. Nobody would fall through the cracks or be forgotten. If I wanted to copy a large number of email addresses for an email I wanted to send, I could do that.

This spreadsheet system shot us out of a cannon. Each day you could see who is set to be contacted. I included a space where you could note what was discussed or how we communicated. It was all there.

If we missed out on a new household who decided against insuring with our agency, we would input their information. Then, about a year later, we could reach out to them to try and earn their business again.

We worked this program consistently. It resulted in our agency leading the entire company in new household acquisitions.

I have given talks and presentations to agencies all over the country. This started to catch on in many other agencies as well. It was a way to be more organized and consistent.

Our corporate office tied this program into the agency operating system, where we manage our clients. It does make it a bit easier than having the spreadsheet, but there are still agents that tell me they still use the spreadsheet system I developed.

A system like this can be used for any business. All businesses quote or give proposals to prospective customers all the time. Nobody wins 100% of the proposals they give.

If you miss out on a customer, what follow up program do you have? The money that you spent on marketing and advertising obviously made them contact you. Maybe someone referred them to you. If you swing and miss, step back up to the plate and swing again. Recontact them. Ask if you can try to earn their business again. Trust me, you'll be one of the few that do.

Put those quoted, proposed, and not-sold customer contacts in a handy systematic follow up system. The same can go for recapturing old clients. Reach out. It costs nothing other than time. It's much cheaper than all the money you're spending on marketing to new, prospective customers. You already have people you've worked with. Swing and swing until they tell you that you've struck out. Go down swinging!

Winning Back Old Clients

All businesses lose clients. It could be due to pricing, poor customer experience, lack of support, or any number of reasons. Some clients you're sad to see go, while others maybe you're not so sad. As much as you try, you can't please everyone all the time. But it's still hard to watch good clients leave.

Once they do leave, what's your plan to get them back? Do you have a plan to get them back? Or are you just going to give up and not try to ever get back the good clients?

What most overlook is once that client decides to leave, your chance of ever getting them back is based upon how you reacted to them leaving. The reaction will determine if they ever do business with you again.

What has been the reaction when you have left a company that you did business with?

What was that company's reaction like? Would you ever do business with them again?

Winning back clients starts the day they leave you. When you're notified a client is leaving what do you do? Do you argue or create a hostile and bad experience? Or do you thank them for their past business and tell them if anything changes, they're always welcome back?

We do two things whenever we lose a client.

First, we send them a letter breaking down all the

products and services they had with our firm. We state what they were receiving from us. We'll list any benefits or things that they won't be able to get back anymore. This letter also thanks them and mentions that they're welcome to come back.

Second, we send a handwritten thank you card. People have a multitude of options nowadays of who they do business with. We thank them and show our appreciation for the years they had their business with us.

They don't know it yet, but those two things begin the first steps in our client recapture process.

Recapturing old clients is much easier than finding brand new clients. Many clients over the years leave for various reasons only to realize the grass isn't always greener somewhere else. Past clients already know what to expect from you and your firm. If you're offering top notch customer service and creating positive customer experiences, people will come back for your product or service.

It's the value that you provide that will keep clients coming back to you. That's why it's never worth it to burn bridges. If people leave for whatever reason don't hold a grudge. Thank them and tell them they're always welcome back if things change. You'll be surprised how many times things do change and people come back on their own.

What about the past clients you'd like back that don't come back on their own. How do you win them back? Here is what we do:

Identify who. You aren't going to want every client that leaves to come back. We run a list to see who left in the past year that we would like back. They're then added to our ongoing client recapture program.

The longer a past client is gone the harder it will be to get them back. As I discussed earlier, the highest retention tenure for our clients is once they reach five years with us. We use this data to assume that other businesses have a similar retention period, so we want to try and get that client back during the lowest retention period. That gives us 1 to 3 years to win them back. This is why we begin reaching out right at the one year point. The honeymoon period with their new company is over and we want to try and earn their business again.

Why did they leave? One of the most important notes to take when someone informs you that they're leaving your firm is why. What's the reason? Then be sure you note it in their file so that when you are working on recapturing them you can see the reason they left in the first place. This is also vital information for training and improving upon your programs and efficiency in your business. It gives insight into what isn't working and what can be better.

What will be the message? To spur a past client's interest in returning, you need to make it clear why they should come back. What's changed? What's improved? What would make you come back? Create curiosity. Craft your message around what you want to convey to them.

Contact them. The hardest part in your recapture program is getting in touch with the client again. We operate a consistent touch program with everyone the following ways at specific timeframes in the 1-to-3-year recapture period after they left.

First, we try to find a way to run into them in person.

This allows us to have a conversation. Second, we'll make a phone call and send out a text to them. Third, we'll send a personalized email, handwritten letter, and postcard. By using these different approaches, it allows us to convey the message we want to send them and touch them multiple ways.

Be consistent. Make sure you and your team have a formal program set and stick with it.

Once a client leaves they still receive our popular newsletter and our annual letter which I mentioned in Part 1. This allows us to keep in contact with them even if they're no longer a client. These are both highly informative beyond just the business they had with us. That's why many still appreciate getting these and don't unsubscribe.

Work on increasing your client return rate. Maintain persistence in your recapture program and remember that it all begins the day they leave with how you react to them leaving. When a client leaves and then returns, odds are they aren't leaving again.

20
Breaking Records

Our agency has set and broken several records through the years. The most prized record we broke was in 2016. That year we decided we wanted to break the company record for the most life insurance policies written in a year. At the time the record was held by an Arizona agency with 194 policies.

So, we said let's go! Let's be the first to ever hit 200! We finished with 201 policies. How did we do it? That is a question I'm still asked to this day. Let's go back and see.

On December 29, 2015 my team and I sat huddled around our conference table. We were just completing our review of the year. We'd just had our best year in our history. We set agency records for the most revenue, most policies in force, the most new families ever brought in, and set the Wisconsin state record for the most life insurance policies written in a year.

On the agenda, I left "2016 Goals" blank, intentionally. I wanted to see what our team had in mind.

Once we came to that point of the meeting. I asked the question, "What should be our goals for 2016?"

Everyone looked at each other and they all agreed, let's break the company record for the most life insurance policies in a year. We just broke the state record, now let's take down the company record.

I was ecstatic. My team said what I was thinking.

After we knew we were going to break the state record in early December, I really wanted to go after the company record. I didn't say a word. It turns out my team had the same line of thinking. If that isn't a sign of a great team, that thinks in lock-step with you, I don't know what is.

We set our sights on 200. Let's break the record and be the first agency to ever cross into 200. With the current record at 194 policies we knew it was going to be a huge mountain to climb. How were we going to get to 200 and break the most coveted record in American Family?

The first thing we had to do was break it down, so the 200 doesn't sound so daunting.

If you've sold life insurance, you are aware that not everyone that wants it will qualify for it. They must be in good enough health to be approved. It's possible they get outright declined or that their price is rated up for a health condition etc.

To hit 200 we knew that we would have to actually write about 235. In our research we realized that we were placing about 85% of the life insurance that we had taken an application for. That made the actual goal 235 policies.

Breaking that down we knew that is about 20 per month, about 5 per week. Well, if that is five per week, then that is one policy per workday. We just took the daunting figure of 235, broke it down and now that number is one. One policy per day Monday through

Friday.

Our next step was to figure out how we were going to be able to talk to enough people to get to that number of sales. Where were those conversations going to come from?

We needed to find a lot of families to talk with. The old game plan for prospecting families wouldn't cut it. So, we changed our approach. During our insurance reviews, we adjusted when we spoke about life insurance.

Current families who had life insurance with us already were contacted by phone and email to review their policies. Did their needs change? Were there gaps where they now need more coverage? Was there a birth of a child or did they get married? Are there options on their current policy to be taken advantage of?

Our new client checklist that we use when onboarding a new family was adjusted when we spoke about life insurance.

We ran a list of all our families in our agency who had homeowner's insurance with us, but had no life insurance. All those customers were mailed a letter, emailed, and called.

Everyone on our team put a sticky note on the bottom of their computer screen that read, "Life." This trained them to remember to ask everyone about it.

As people called in with questions or changes, we made sure we asked them about life insurance. That note was their reminder.

Over the years many have asked how we did it. How the heck did we write that many life insurance policies? That was how. There was no magic potion. It took a lot of hard work and teamwork.

During some weeks we wrote none. But we knew damn well when we came back the next week, we needed to write ten to get back on pace and we did.

I had a monetary incentive for everyone on our team if we broke the record as well. If we achieved it, everyone on the team was going to celebrate together. This was an all-in approach. If you set team goals, everyone on your team should have a say and know they have a role to play in achieving it.

The most important piece was our mindset and consistency. You must ask. You need to train yourself and your team to ask. Whether they are calling in to speak with me, my sales manager, right on down the line to our phone concierge, they're going to be asked about life insurance. Train yourself and everyone on your team to ask.

We achieved our goal on December 28th.

21
A Legacy of Thank You

Coming out of high school, being an athlete, a "jock", I had a bit of the attitude that I was better than other people. Like everyone, however, once you graduate and walk out those high school or college doors you realize that you're just like everyone else. What you did in school means nothing anymore. You're responsible for charting your own life course.

Am I going to be a lazy bum or am I going to change the world? Can I change an industry and make an impact? Will I lead groups and teams of people? What type of impact will I make? Those are real life questions that hit you once you are exposed to the real world.

Dan Jorndt closed his email to me with, "Thank you, thank you. Thank the good people (and parents, wife, friends) over and over and over again. Good people and good works can never be recognized too much." It stuck with me the most. It's something that has shaped how I speak and associate with people in both business and society. I think it made me a better person.

So, ask yourself. When was the last time you told someone thank you? When was the last time someone said thank you to you? The phrase thank you, I think, has been lost a bit. Why is that?

Every phone call or in person meeting I have with a

client, I speak those words to them at the end. When I buy something, I tell whoever helped me or takes my money at the cash register thank you. I've had conversations with upset clients and at the end of those calls I still tell them thank you. Clients who've left my agency, I still thank for all the years they had business with me.

Treat others how you would want to be treated. Sometimes I may be a bit overboard on saying thank you to people, but I don't care. Life is too short to burn bridges.

Over the years Dan and I have conversed via email and mail. I shared the success that came after he sent me his email and how it helped me chart my path. He even mailed me his Walgreens book publication "*Have a Great Week*" which was a collection he had done of his Monday morning jolts to his Walgreens team.

To say Dan was more than gracious is an understatement. He took the time to converse and help a stumbling 20-year-old kid in sales get his footing. I will forever be grateful to him. It speaks to his character.

When you receive tips from someone like this you feel an obligation to listen to what he says. You don't want to fail or let him down. That has been in the back of my mind since that day. I told him that in my most recent letter to him. He pushed me without me even being an employee of his at Walgreens. Some people, I've learned, are leaders in both business and life. Dan Jorndt is one of those people, and for that, Dan, thank you! I'm forever grateful for the selfless and kind human being that you are.

Hopefully someday someone gets in touch with me

to share the impact I had on their life.

That is a life goal that everyone should have.

Dan never even bought anything from me. You can make all the money in the world and have all the greatest things in it, but what impact did you make on others? How will you be remembered? How do you think I will remember Dan Jordnt? For me, it won't be for leading Walgreens.

Great people are not isolated, they've had many people contribute to their greatness. The greatest have recognized that, and thanked the many that came before them. Will you leave any lasting legacy with people after you're dead and gone? Strive for greatness. Strive to be remembered as that great person people talk about, because of the impact you had on others long after you're gone.

Closing Remarks

The Train of Life

At birth, we boarded the train of life and met our parents. We believed that they would always travel by our side. However, at some station, our parents would step down from the train, leaving us on life's journey alone.

As time goes by, some significant people will board the train: siblings, children, friends, and even the love of our life.

Many will step down and leave a seat that no one else will be able to fill. Others will go so unnoticed that we won't realize that they vacated their seats! This train ride has been a mixture of joy, sorrow, fantasy, expectations, hellos, goodbyes, and farewells.

A successful journey consists of having a good relationship with all passengers, requiring that we give the best of ourselves. The mystery that prevails is that we do not know at which station we ourselves will step down. Thus, we must try to travel along the track of life in the best possible way -- loving, forgiving, giving, and sharing.

When the time comes for us to step down and leave our seat empty, we should leave behind beautiful memories for those who continue to travel on the train.

I wish you a joyful journey on the train of life. Reap success and give lots of love. More importantly, thank

God for the journey.

Thank you for being one of the passengers on my train.

Eric Soda

Appendix

Hot Takes

Take the path less traveled. Be different. Don't be afraid to try something new. If you fail, try again. You know the adage, you miss every shot you don't take. Some of the best returns came from ideas I almost gave up on. Be a contrarian. An overused path becomes a rut. "Go instead where there is no path and leave a trail." (Ralph Waldo Emerson)

Loyalty is a two-way street. Be sure you're spending time with clients who value your time and what you have to offer. Your product or service shouldn't be suitable and right for everyone.

Allocate your time and energy to the clients that you want to work with and the clients who want to work with you. Don't ever be afraid to say no and walk away from anyone who does not value you as much as you value them.

You're only as good as the team around you. Don't be afraid to delegate. Don't be afraid to replace yourself. You need to learn this early. The sooner you do this the sooner you will thank yourself. Give up control and let your teammates help you. That is why you hired them, right?

Everyone has to start somewhere. There is no substitute for hard work. If you think that right out of school or your first day on the job, you're going to be the boss, you're mistaken. We all need to learn by gaining knowledge and experience. Everyone has to put their time in. Anything worth building will take sacrifice. It will start with stress, anxiety, and sleepless nights, but your trading short term struggle for long term gain.

Scouring social media wastes an immeasurable amount of time. Forget the fear of missing out. Looking back, I am sick to my stomach with the vast number of hours I've spent wasting time on social media. A complete waste of time mindlessly scrolling. It's like a disease we've all contracted. What if we shut off from Twitter, Facebook, Instagram, and TikTok for a day, week, or month? What would you do? Think about that. What would you really do? Would you read, write a book, start a blog, create works of art, finally start that business you've always wanted?

Make time for what matters most. Think for a minute. What is on your bucket list? Now, instead of wasting it on this or that, start creating action steps to get closer to an item on that list. Go after the most attainable thing today. Or go after the top and most outrageous thing. Either way get off your ass and pick your head up from your screen and do the work. Create something great.

Leave a legacy in print. Pass it on. What if you died unexpectedly? How would your family and children remember you? What if you could help them through life, even if you were dead?

Write an ongoing memoir. What can they learn from your mistakes and successes to be better and even more successful than you?

Say Thank You. Be a kind person. Say thank you. Humble yourself and be appreciative of all people. No matter their race, color, political beliefs, opinions, or whatever somebody else thinks, be grateful to them and for them. Don't forget that because I think we do today more than ever.

Favorite Books

You ask what books are the best? I've provided a list of 25 books that I feel would be beneficial to you. These are the books that had a tremendous impact on me. I found these at various points in my life. And no, I do not have a favorite book. I indicate what book I have given the most as a gift and my most read book.

The 7 Habits of Highly Effective People: Powerful Lessons in Personal Change by Stephen Covey

Bird by Bird: Some Instructions on Writing and Life by Anne Lamott

Chase the Lion: If Your Dream Doesn't Scare You, It's Too Small by Mark Batterson

Common Sense Investing by John Bogle

Essentialism: The Disciplined Pursuit of Less by Greg McKeown (My Most Read Book)

Every Day I Fight: Making a Difference, Kicking Cancer's Ass by Stuart Scott

Good to Great: Why Some Companies Make the Leap and Others Don't by Jim Collins

Hell Yeah or No: What's Worth Doing by Derek Sivers (My Most Gifted Book)

How I Raised Myself from Failure to Success in Selling by Frank Bettger

How to Win Friends and Influence People by Dale Carnegie

Man's Search for Meaning by Viktor Frankl

Outliers: The Story of Success by Malcolm Gladwell

Shoe Dog: A Memoir by the Creator of Nike by Phil Knight

Steve Jobs by Walter Isaacson

The Last Lecture by Randy Pausch

The Millionaire Next Door: The Surprising Secrets of America's Wealthy by Thomas Stanley & William Dank

The Power of Positive Thinking by Norman Vincent Peale

The Pursuit of Happyness by Chris Gardner

The Richest Man in Babylon by George Clason

The Snowball: Warren Buffett and the Business of Life by Alice Schroeder

The War of Art: Break Through the Blocks and Win Your Inner Creative Battles by Steven Pressfield

The Why Cafe by John Strelecky

Think and Grow Rich by Napoleon Hill

Tools of Titans: The Tactics, Routines, and Habits of Billionaires, Icons, and World-Class Performers by Tim Ferriss

Tribe of Mentors: Short Life Advice from the Best in the World by Tim Ferriss

When Breath Becomes Air by Paul Kalanithi

About the Author

Eric Soda is an author, entrepreneur and investor. He owns one of the largest insurance agencies in the country for the Fortune 500 company that his agency represents. His team has been nationally recognized for its achievements and company sales records. Eric has presented to businesses all over the country on ways to improve their sales, service and overall operations. He's also the author of the popular blog, *Spilled Coffee*. He lives in Neenah, Wisconsin with his wife and two kids.

You can connect with Eric on:
Twitter @ericsoda

Subscribe to his blog:
Spilledcoffee.substack.com